D0597367

Volume 1

understanding human behavior

An Illustrated Guide to Successful Human Relationships

COLUMBIA HOUSE / New York

Editor	Nicolas Wright
Deputy Editor	Susan Joiner
Senior Designer	Stewart Cowley
Art Editor	Mary Cooper
Art Assistant	Jeff Gurney
Editorial Assistants	Mundy Ellis
	Sarie Forster
	John Moore
	Michael McIntyre
Picture Research	Diane Rich
	Hazel Robinson
	Paul Snelgrove
Editorial Director	Graham Donaldson

Production Manager: Warren E. Bright
Cover Design: Harry W. Fass

© BPC Publishing Limited 1974
Distributed by Columbia House, 51 West 52nd Street, New York, New York 10019

editorial board

Dr. Bernard Camber is a psychiatrist and a Fellow of the Medical Research Council, a Fellow of the Rockefeller Institute and a Research Fellow of the College of Physicians and Surgeons of Columbia University, New York.

Dr. William C. Dement is recognized as a world authority on sleep. He is Director of the Sleep Disorders Clinic and Laboratory at Stanford University Medical Center, California.

Christine Doyle has been a medical correspondent since 1967. She has also worked for many medical publishers and medical journals, including *World Medicine.*

Dr. Christopher Evans is an experimental psychologist and Secretary of the Brain Research Association, and author of articles on cybernetics, psychical research, dreaming and scientology.

Professor H. J. Eysenck is Director of the Department of Psychology at the University of London. He is well known for his sometimes controversial research into the field of personality and intelligence.

Professor Harry F. Harlow is a past President of the American Psychological Association and has been a scientific adviser for the Government.

Brian Inglis is a well-known author, broadcaster and journalist. His books include *Revolution in Medicine; Drugs, Doctors and Disease; Fringe Medicine* and *A History of Medicine.*

Dr. T. B. Mulholland is a noted authority on brain waves and biofeedback research. He majored in psychology at Tufts College, then took his M.A. and Ph.D. in experimental psychology from Clark University in Worcester, Massachusetts.

Tony Osman is a science editor and once taught science in a progressive coeducational school and a private school. He has written many film, television and radio scripts and is the author of *In Aid of Surgery.*

Dr. Eric Trimmer is the author of a highly successful series of books on family health which have won him international acclaim. As well as being in general practice he is also the Medical Editor of *Medical News,* a magazine for doctors, and the Editor of *British Journal of Sexual Medicine.* He is a Fellow of the Royal Society of Medicine.

contents

Marshall Cavendish

introduction

Since time began man has restlessly sought the answers to an endless list of questions concerning that most fascinating of subjects—himself. What makes him think and act the way he does? Why does he love one person yet hate another? Why are some people aggressive, others submissive?

Understanding Human Behavior has been designed to help solve the mystery. Its main purpose is to entertain and inform the reader in a new, crisp and compelling manner. Textbook dryness has no place in the series but at the same time it is presented in an academically responsible and authoritative way.

In our determination to sift the significant from the superficial high standards have been set. These will be maintained by using contributors and consultants who believe—as we do—that it is possible, and indeed essential, to communicate knowledge in lucid and vital terms.

To sustain the interest of the reader, heighten his awareness of his role as an individual and his place in society, each volume is broken down into seven sections. These are as follows:

1. *Mind and Body:* How the brain and body interact, the bodily processes that make activity or behavior possible. We explain in detail the complex workings of the brain; our physiological needs and urges such as hunger, thirst and sex; our senses—smell, touch, hearing, vision; the physical changes associated with pregnancy, adolescence and old age and the way in which they affect our behavior.

2. *The Individual:* Each person is a unique individual, a product of his particular heredity and environment. Here we look at some of the factors which produce these differences—the most obvious of which are personality and intelligence. We explain what makes a person behave the way he does: the psychopath, the alcoholic, the Don Juan or the compulsive gambler.

3. *Human Relationships:* No man is an island. We are born into a family and in turn form our own. We are concerned here with our closest human relationships—sexual attraction, falling in love, marriage, parent-child relationships.

4. *Man in Society:* Two's company and three's a crowd. We are all members of society yet each of us is affected differently by social attitudes. Do we behave differently in groups? What forms our political attitudes? Are men more dominant than women? These are just

(continued)

some of the questions we will be answering.

5. *Changing View of Man:* Throughout history there have been men who have contributed greatly to the advancement of man's thought about and understanding of himself: men such as Darwin, Freud, Jung and Pavlov. And more recently, Kinsey, B. F. Skinner and Benjamin Spock. You will meet them all in *Understanding Human Behavior.*

6. *Question and Answer:* Here you will find the answers to all the questions you've ever wanted to ask about sexual behavior, stress, psychotherapy, mental illness, intelligence, these and many more . . .

7. *Self-Improvement:* This section directly involves the reader in such areas as increasing his memory power, speeding his reading ability, overcoming shyness and improving his vocabulary.

This first volume of *Understanding Human Behavior* begins with dreams and the strange world of sleep. Why do we dream and what do our dreams mean? Are they, as man once believed, glimpses of the future? Or do dreams reflect our innermost feelings? What happens if we are deprived of dreams? Volume One solves some of the mysteries and gives you a completely new insight into what happens when your unconscious mind takes over.

Are you an extrovert or an introvert? Do you like going to parties, driving fast cars and generally looking for excitement? Or would you rather stay at home and lead a quiet life? Discover the kind of personality you really are. We all want to be thought attractive by the opposite sex. But is this really necessary? Do we worry too much about the way we look?

Volume One of *Understanding Human Behavior* contains many other fascinating and informative articles. These include a study of man's aggressive instinct; an in-depth examination of stress; what dictates our choice of marriage partner; a discussion on whether men are more clever than women—or vice versa—and why falling in love sometimes proves a wild goose chase.

This is merely the beginning. Each successive volume will enrich and enhance your knowledge. Above all, this series is concerned with people and the fact that every one of us is a unique individual.

—The Editor

Brian Froud

The need to dream

Researchers are beginning to solve some of the mysteries that surround our dreams. Experimental work has shown the disturbing physical and mental effects on subjects deprived of dream-sleep. But what do our dreams mean? The psychoanalysts have some answers. For example, when a person dreams of being naked in public it could mean a fear of displaying innermost feelings.

Dreams have been a favorite subject of poets and philosophers for centuries. Only recently, however, have scientists and researchers begun to pierce this mysterious world and discover the first clues to answering the simplest and yet most intriguing of questions surrounding this universal phenomenon.

Everybody dreams, though not everybody is able to remember having done so; and we are beginning to know now not only when and for how long we dream, but also why. And experiments have demonstrated that when an individual is deprived—not of *sleep*—but of dream-sleep, it has catastrophic effects on mental and physical health.

What, then, of the substance of our dreams? What about the strange cast of characters which emerge to play out their dramas on the stage of sleep? Some seem to be members of our families, past and living; others friends; many appear total strangers. Then there are animals, weird settings, situations at once familiar and yet hauntingly bizarre and even disturbing.

Here, too, scientific signposts exist which point to some explanation of what these characters *really* symbolize, and why we may have a particular dream at a particular time. We know also that dreams may be able to tell us something helpful about ourselves; about our deepest fears and most secret wishes which may be affecting our behavior without our conscious knowledge.

Flickering Eyes

First, how do we know how much of our sleep is occupied by dreams, and why we *need* to dream? Research by an eminent physiologist, Professor Nathaniel Kleitman, has demonstrated that during sleep there are periods when our eyes flick backwards and forwards under closed lids as though we were watching the action of a play. In fact by arousing subjects while observing these movements (called Rapid Eye Movement), Kleitman established that REMs always accompanied a dream period.

Further experiments by Kleitman and other researchers have indicated not only that REMs are a sign that the subject is dreaming—following with his eyes the pictorial development of the "dream story"—but also that REMs last from two to ten minutes in the early part of the night and, as morning approaches, become much longer, some lasting for as long as an hour.

So quite a considerable amount of our total sleep is spent dreaming, a phenomenon that seems to be essential as well as normal. Once the scientists knew when someone was dreaming they were able to set up experiments in which subjects were awakened just as soon as REMs were detected.

The results of these deliberate dream-deprivation experiments proved quite startling.

After a relatively short time the subjects began having daydreams, mild hallucinations, and suffered from considerable disorientation. The longer the period of deprivation, the

1. Deprivation Dreams

Sex dreams are obviously linked with deprivation. Dreaming about food if you are on a diet or smoking if you have given it up are clear cases of deprivation. Such dreams indicate that the habit or urge, although overcome consciously, has not been thoroughly repressed.

2. Anxiety Dreams

Dreams in which you have lost something important represent anxiety although the subject of the dream is not necessarily the cause of your anxiety. If, for example, you lost your wallet this could indicate worry about your own or your husband's job. If it was your passport perhaps you are anxious about your identity. If in your dreams you have not carried out some important task, it could be that you are taking on too much. Another common anxiety dream is one of taking examinations, or being interviewed. This represents a fear of being judged and found wanting and could occur at "testing" times in your life.

3. Sexual Dreams

You may find yourself in a sexual situation with a most unlikely person. This could be someone you stood next to in the elevator, or an acquaintance you do not overtly desire. Possibly this person attracts you at an unconscious level or perhaps represents someone more significant in your life who is at the same time forbidden. Sex dreams can also be necessary for physical relief. The wet dream of adolescents is an obvious example. People who undergo periods of sexual abstinence are likely to have sex dreams.

4. Prophetic Dreams

You dream about something that later takes place—a long lost friend writes to you, or appears on your doorstep. Does this suggest that some kind of extrasensory communication has occurred? In most cases it seems doubtful, although psychologists are now investigating such phenomena scientifically.

5. Flying Dreams

Dreams where you appear to be floating effortlessly indicate escape. When, however, there is some effort involved in your flying, rather as if you were swimming breaststroke, this could represent ambition or striving. Falling, or losing height, could mean a return to reality, or that you have been overambitious.

6. Terror Nightmares

In this dream you are being pursued by some "thing." You have no idea what it is but are terrified just the same. You find that you are unable to run away—perhaps your limbs become rigid—but you always wake up just before the terror gets you. This dream could represent some part of yourself that frightens you. Maybe you have an aggressive or sexual wish which is unacceptable to your conscious mind. And because perhaps it is a strong, deep-seated wish you cannot escape from it.

more severe these symptoms became, until these experiments had to be abandoned for fear of permanently damaging the mental and physical health of the subjects.

A few years ago Peter Tripp, a New York disk jockey, kept himself awake eight days for charity. He sat in the window of a Times Square store, and there — for every passer-by to witness — was the gradual but inexorable descent of one individual of sound mind and body through initial confusion to final mania. Following this stunt, Tripp suffered a three-month depression. It seems the longest a human being can survive without REM sleep is ten days. After that permanent mental disability — and eventual death — will follow.

But why should dreaming be so vital? To answer that we have to ask some more questions. What *is* a dream? Where does it come from? Who writes the scripts and assembles the characters which our eyes follow so diligently behind their closed lids? How can we be in the dream and watching it at the same time?

Try to remember a few of your dreams; enter that dream world for a moment, if you can, and think of a few things that seem to be common to most dreams. At the time, they seem very real. But that reality often bears no relation to the waking world. In our dreams we can be all-powerful. We can fly; we can scorn convention; we can ignore morality; we can meet with presidents, kings and queens; we can fall from great heights without harm; we can have illicit affairs without scruple and we can experience both fear and ecstasy to a degree unlikely in real life. In a dream, wrote Plato, a man may mate his own mother. In a dream, the Bible tells us, young Joseph had his entire family, including his dead mother, bowing and kow-towing to him.

Holiday from Reality

It is almost as if the dream is some kind of holiday, an escape from everyday restraints, from the moralities, conventions and social niceties that all of us have to observe to some extent. Freud, the first man who seriously attempted to solve the mystery of dreams, suggested that they were, in fact, a kind of safety valve; a way of giving expression — but in a disguised way — to feelings and emotions which, because they are so antisocial or simply too awful to contemplate, we have locked away

4.

5.

6.

Brian Froud

in the depths of our unconscious.

The mind. as Freud saw it, is not only a mechanism for thought, but a vessel containing feelings and emotions ranging from the most gentle and loving to the most violent. Now some of these feelings, of hatred, of jealousy, perhaps of extraordinary meanness, which compose our total personality are so beyond the pale of acceptable human behavior that the individual dare not even acknowledge their existence.

So our conscience—or what Freud called the super ego—keeps these feelings banished in the depths of our unconscious. There, in the darkest dungeons of the mind, they seethe away, prisoners seeking their escape. There, in another inner reality, they exist just as surely as the feelings of which we are consciously aware and indirectly affect our behavior.

Shameful Vice

For example a man who believes that meanness is a particularly shameful vice—that it does not "bear thinking about"—may in fact himself be extremely mean at heart. But because of his attitude this feeling has never been permitted to reach consciousness. He never becomes aware of his inner feelings but is forced to pay a high price for his ignorance.

Only by publicly putting his hand in his pocket can he hide from himself what is in his heart. He becomes the man in the bar who is always embarrassingly eager to pour drinks down the throat of the slightest acquaintance while his wife says:

"I can't understand him. He buys drinks all around, but resents buying the kids a bar of chocolate."

And he complains: "People take advantage because I'm so generous." He is angry at being exploited but helpless to prevent it. The psychoanalysts would say he is suffering from a repression.

Now dreams, suggested Freud, are an expression of repressed emotions, of our innermost fears and desires. While we sleep these influential specters arise to haunt the battlements of the mind, pressing upward to find expression in the action of the dream. There, the mean man may gloat over his meanness; there we are prey to the "unthinkable" terror; there we may give reign to our desires for unlimited power and sexual behavior free from the constraints of morality.

However, even in the dream, these fears and desires are expressed in symbolic form. The characters and situations are not what they seem. A father, perceived as a stern, authoritarian figure, in a dream may appear in the guise of a judge, a policeman or a teacher. A dream in which we are taking examinations or being interviewed may reflect anxiety and lack of security in a real-life work situation.

The value of dreaming, therefore, apart from that of providing psychoanalysts and psychiatrists with clues to possible underlying causes of seriously disturbed behavior in an individual, is that it is an avenue of escape for feelings that demand expression but which cannot be expressed in outer reality.

Without that release, as experiments have shown, these feelings begin to intrude on our waking life in the form of fantasies and hallucinations until the mind is unable to exercise any control over these "unruly" elements of our personality. If a government cannot exercise law and order, if there is such dissension within its own ranks that it can no longer maintain a united front and act with authority, the result is breakdown and anarchy.

If the human personality cannot control its own "dissident" elements, it, too, begins to break down, and the result is manic behavior. Normally a government tolerates a certain amount of dissent from its own supporters; indeed a government probably would not be considered "healthy" if it did not allow differences to be expressed.

Outward Unity

But if the dissidents go too far, they will probably be banished from the government altogether—and so, too, with the personality, which outwardly presents a unity but which is in fact composed of conflicting elements.

Deprived of any opportunities for dreaming the personality begins to degenerate into disorder; and because none of us is without repressed fears and desires our dreams are usually quite normal and certainly necessary.

Indeed much of humanity shares these fears and desires, and research has shown that there are standard dream situations common to millions. The illustrations cover a selection of "standard" dreams with which you may well be familiar.

A typical night's sleep (top) shows dream (paradoxical) sleep and orthodox sleep. In orthodox sleep (left) brain activity is slow, eye movements few, throat muscles tense, and heartbeat is regular. In dreaming (right) the brain is much busier, eye movements become rapid, throat muscles are relaxed, and the heartbeat is irregular.

0 1 2 3 4 5 6 7 HOURS

Wakefulness

Paradoxical Sleep

Orthodox Sleep

ORTHODOX SLEEP big slow waves

electro-encephalogram

eyes quiescent
(small transmitted brain potentials seen)

throat muscles tense
(innumerable small electrical spikes from muscle

heart regular

PARADOXICAL SLEEP low voltage waves

electro-encephalogram

eyes rapid movements

throat muscles relaxed

heart irregular

Ralph Waldo Emerson, the essayist and philosopher, said, "A skillful man reads his dreams for his self-knowledge." Each night, you dream at least once and probably three or four times. Some people remember their dreams in detail but most of us forget them within a few minutes. It is difficult to interpret a single dream, but often the same theme will reoccur. Leave a notebook and pencil by your bed (a tape recorder is even better) and write what you remember each morning for at least two weeks—the longer you keep it up the more information you will get. When you have written down or recorded all that remains in your mind, add the date, and leave it unread for another two weeks. You may find file index cards or plain postcards more convenient than a notebook.

Inner Reality

Your dreams reflect your inner reality, hidden attitudes, fears and wishes—you are the best person to interpret them in the light of your life as it actually is. When you first read through your series of dreams, some themes may become immediately apparent—a particular character, or type, may pursue you through different situations; a landscape may be recurrent. To help sift the varying contents of your dreams, use the following classifications.

Setting: This may portray the ways in which you look at the world. If you feel that the world is closing in on you, you may dream of cramped, confined places. This could be a temporary feeling, related to specific frustrations, or a more general need to escape, expand, seek new opportunities. The setting may be beautiful but dangerous, a rolling landscape with perilous ravines. Again, the setting could be normal, indicating a level of acceptance and relative content. To know whether a particular setting is significant, you would need to keep records over some considerable time—six months or a year.

Characters: Relatives, friends or acquaintances? Apart from yourself, who figures in your dreams? It is likely to be the people close to you, but we know that strangers and peripheral characters often invade your night world. What could they stand for? Let your thoughts roam freely around the people who appear. One woman, in the months following her father's death, dreamed, not of him, but of an old classmate she had not seen for years. This puzzled her until she remembered that the other girl's

New York disk jockey Peter Tripp went without sleep for eight days as a charity stunt. He suffered a resulting three-months' depression.

father had died while she was at school, and the other children had been much struck by the event. Examine carefully the qualities displayed by your dream people. Who do they remind you of? Who have you had the same feelings toward?

Plot: Some dreams have a strong narrative line. You may seem to be in the cinema watching a drama in which you are not involved. What is the nature of the interaction? Hostility is common. Who is the aggressor? What is the outcome? What of friendly contact? You can gain considerable insight into your suppressed fears and wishes by analyzing these events. Are you being blocked or frustrated in some way? Or are you powerful in dreams? In men, sexual dreams are common, but not always overt. One man dreamed of a lady plumber turn-

ing on a faucet for him and awoke to find that he had ejaculated. A woman, instructed under hypnotic suggestion to dream of homosexuality, reported that she had entered a "ladies only" compartment in a train. Events mean different things to different people—you must apply what you know of your own life.

Emotion: Often, the events of a dream fade quickly, leaving you with an impression of emotional tone. Apprehension and anxiety account for 40 percent of dream feelings, showing that most people have a considerable, though normal, level of anxiety. In times of particular stress, this would increase. Did you know consciously that you were worried? Can you think of a possible cause? It is less trying to face fears rather than pretend they do not exist. Anger, happiness and excitement account for about 18 percent each of studied dreams. What is the predominant feeling of your dreams? How is it related to your life? Only you can tell!

13

Dreams explained

Have you ever dreamed about airplanes, taking a journey, cats or dancing? If you have, do you understand their meaning? Our A to Z of dream symbols will give you a new insight into the strange world of sleep. Do you dream in color? How long do your dreams last? Does eating cheese give you nightmares? We answer these and other questions.

Once, men believed that dreams were glimpses of the future, visions of a world in which the boundaries of time had collapsed. Others believed that they were memories of the nightly adventures of the soul or spirit which during sleep was freed from the shackles of the physical world. But it was left to Sigmund Freud to produce the first real insight into their significance. He realized that their role was not mystical but severely practical, sending man messages from his unconscious mind.

Keys to the Unconscious

Our true motives, he argued, could be determined more readily by the study of our dreams than of our conscious thoughts. The weird nature of dream material he explained by introducing the notion of "disguise." This can be explained as follows:

In many cases the messages from the unconscious are simple and therefore appear in the dream in straightforward fashion—for example a man who is having difficulties with his wife will probably dream about quarreling with her. Occasionally, however, the raw material of the dream may be more threatening. Let us suppose that the man really hates his wife and yet denies this even to himself. In such cases some part of the unconscious mind "senses" and "disguises" the psychologically distressing contents of the dream so that they appear in "symbolic" form. Freud said that this was to prevent an unpleasant dream from waking the sleeper.

In psychoanalysis, therefore, part of the strategy is to examine the symbolic content of the dream and attempt to interpret it to establish its *true* meaning. Once the patient can

see the messages from his unconscious for what they really are, he can then take steps to act on them. This ingenious theory of course provides a framework for the interpretation of all dreams—when they are straightforward the message is taken as "read." When the meaning is unclear at first glance, then symbolism must be involved and the dream has to be

This man was probably consciously quite willing to help his wife by washing the dishes. But tonight he may dream of being imprisoned in a cage by a cat who holds the key around its neck. The cat symbolizes his wife, and his dream is an unconscious expression of his resentment and frustration, feelings he might not know he harbors against her.

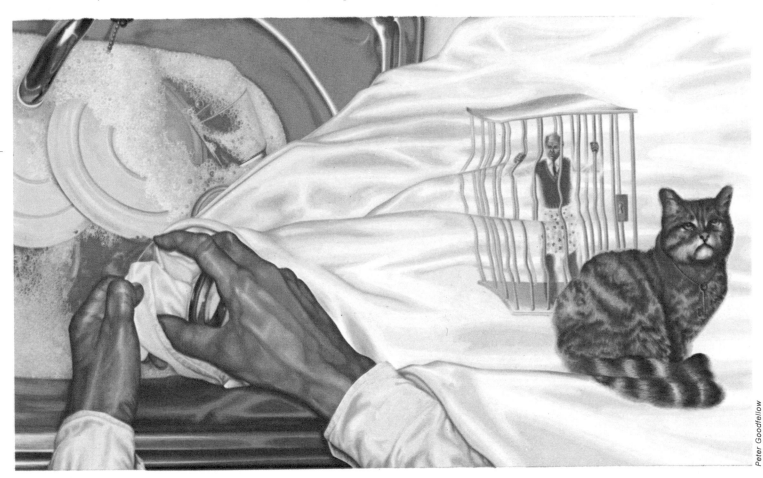

Peter Goodfellow

translated first, then interpreted.

The weakness of the theory of course is that interpretation is largely a matter for the psychoanalyst and his patient and is therefore highly subjective. In fact few hard and fast rules for decoding the symbols exist and even fewer are generally accepted by all schools of psychoanalysis. Followers of Carl Jung, for example, accept the symbolic basis of much of our dream life but propose many radically different interpretations from those of the Freudians.

The highly significant differences in the nature of the Freudian and Jungian interpretations are partly explained by the fact that Freud gathered his material from the case histories of his patients, noticed that certain imagery recurred constantly and "interpreted" the imagery in the light of what he believed were the patient's psychological problems. Jung on the other hand tried to relate the imagery to ancient myths and symbols and therefore decoded the dream in terms of the mythological significance of these images.

Personal Interpretation

But whether one looks at the dream in Freudian or Jungian terms there is still considerable disagreement even among the followers of any single school and thus it is almost impossible to provide a comprehensible catalogue of dream interpretation. With these reservations however the following "A to Z" of dream symbols may serve as a useful guide. Its principal purpose is *not* to allow instant dream interpretation, but rather to give a general sample of the vast range of potential dream symbols and the way in which they are interpreted by psychoanalysts. Bear in mind, however, that, in the final resolution, dream interpretation must be a matter for the individual and his *own* unconscious.

Marshall Cavendish

Dream symbols A-Z

AIRPLANE

In all dream interpretation the "mood" of the dream is of tremendous significance. If the mood is pleasant and relaxed, aircraft can be seen as signs of liberation, denoting contentment and a feeling of general satisfaction. When, as is more often the case, the aircraft appears as an ominous object, the reverse interpretation applies and the dreamer may be aware of a threatening situation building up in his waking life.

BIRD

For thousands of years the bird has been taken as symbolizing a woman, but in more recent psychoanalytic terms can depict the female orgasm. Other interpretations see it as a symbol of peace—the dove is used here—or, possibly, of wisdom. It is interesting to note how frequently the bird features in surrealist paintings, which draw heavily upon dream imagery.

CAT

The essential feminine quality of the cat as an animal inevitably identifies it with women and specifically with a woman close to the dreamer. In mythology the cat has always had magical associations and as much of the Jungian dream interpretation is based on mythology, the cat in Jungian terms may refer to a deep problem of a mystical or spiritual nature, a deep psychological secret.

DANCING

In Freudian terms, dancing may represent sexual intercourse or love-making. Other interpretations stress the joyful features of the dance and also of the sense of liberation that it brings.

EXCREMENT

Curiously, both modern psychologists and the ancient dream interpreters equate excrement with money. Freud in particular believed that a child's obsessive interest in feces was equivalent to the preoccupation that adults show with money. For those who seek ancient origins to dream symbolism, it is worth noting that the Incan expression for gold was "excrement of the gods"!

FISH

According to Freud the fish has a strong sexual significance, with the fish itself probably being equated with the penis. Jungians take a more archetypal point of view, observing that the fish is the symbol of Christianity and of wisdom. Dreaming of fish therefore may denote mental tranquility and perhaps some sort of psychological insight,

GUN

The gun is one of the strongest of sexual symbols denoting both the male erection and the controlled aggression of the sex act. Non-Freudians also tend to accept the sexual interpretation but lay more stress on the gun's implicit associations with power.

HORSE

The horse is another symbol with heavy sexual overtones and denotes the ideal of male virility. Most psychoanalytic schools take horse riding as representing the sexual act and may imply some frustration in the dreamer's love life, whether it is apparent or not.

INCEST

Incestuous dreams turn up frequently in psychoanalysis and are not, strictly speaking, symbolic since they do in fact represent the inevitable sexual ties that exist between parents and children, brothers and sisters. In many dreams, however, the true message may be disguised by the process known as ''reversal'' when an incestuous dream may imply an imminent family quarrel.

JOURNEY

Journeys which are constantly interrupted in an irritating way reveal that the individual is passing through an anxious and frustrating time. A long journey may often refer to the dreamer's life and the nature of the journey reflects his own assessment of how this is progressing. Jungians see journeys as representing important transitional stages in one's life, suggesting that the dreamer is either embarking, or about to embark, on a significant adventure either in love or daily work.

KNIFE

A famous sexual symbol, seen as such by almost all psychoanalysts, and reflecting the underlying aggression of much sexual behavior. The symbolism is particularly dramatic and obvious when the male (in the dream) uses the knife to stab a woman in the stomach.

Marshall Cavendish

The Whys and Wherefores

DO WE DREAM EVERY NIGHT?

Yes, all human beings dream every night for up to a fifth or a quarter of the sleep period. This is even true of people who claim that they never dream—by which they mean either that they never *experience* or never *remember* a dream. Psychologists can tell when people are dreaming by strange movements which are made by their eyes (REMs or Rapid Eye Movements) and also by certain changes in the patterns of their brain waves. In experimental tests, people who claimed never to have dreamed were taken into sleep laboratories and were woken as soon as the REMs appeared. All immediately reported that they had been experiencing a dream, though most were very surprised when they realized this!

WHAT IS A DAYDREAM?

Daydreams are not really related to "night" dreams and the use of the word "dream" in the former case is misleading. Daydreams are consciously controlled fantasies which allow us to plot out a course of action in advance, or explore the various possibilities which are open to us. We may occasionally get "lost" in fantasies, when we suddenly come down to earth with a bump. Daydreams serve a function which may be useful but is completely different from the function of dreams during sleep.

CAN WE DREAM OF EVENTS IN THE FUTURE?

Of course we can, but whether the dreams come true or not is another matter. Scientists have been attempting to study this topic for decades. Almost everyone has heard anecdotes about people who were forewarned in a dream about some disaster, or more simply dreamed of a long lost friend who subsequently turned up the next day. There is no doubt that thousands of stories of this kind have been told, but the dangers of misreporting, exaggeration, errors of memory, and so on are obvious. One of the most famous books written on this topic, *Experiment with Time* by J. W. Dunne, who claimed that most of his dreams foretold the future, has led to a considerable popular interest in the topic, but once again psychologists and scientists have tended to be skeptical of his claims. The most recent experimental work by Drs. Montague Ullman and Stanley Krippner at the Maimonides Hospital in New York claims to have found proof of telepathic and "precognitive" dreams.

I SOMETIMES DREAM OF A FIRE ENGINE RACING ALONG RINGING ITS BELL AND WAKE UP TO FIND THE ALARM CLOCK RINGING. HOW IS THIS?

What happens here is that an ongoing dream (which may be about anything) is interrupted by an alarm or, say, the telephone. This causes the brain to move out of sleep into wakefulness and the conscious mind immediately comes alert. Simultaneously it becomes aware of the dream, which is part of its *internal* world, and the alarm, which is part of the *external* world. For a few seconds it is unable to tell the difference between the two and molds them together as best it can in the form of an amalgamated dream.

DOES EATING CHEESE BRING NIGHTMARES?

Not in itself. Eating cheese or any food in sufficiently large amounts to cause indigestion will often provoke a restless night in which the individual is constantly awakened by complaints from his stomach. This will mean that he is more likely to experience his dreams, many of which will be "colored" by the indigestion and will be nightmares. Equally, an easily digestible snack which impedes stomach contractions during the night can prevent this kind of sleep disturbance and make nightmares less likely. A warm milk drink before retiring can be helpful.

HOW LONG DO DREAMS LAST?

Psychologists now know that we dream for up to a fifth or a quarter of the night but we are unaware of doing so and do not remember most of the dreams. In this sense therefore dreams may last for as much as 30 minutes or an hour, but they would not normally be dreams which we experience. The dream which we talk about when we remember it in the morning is in fact an *interrupted* dream and is only experienced in the transitional period between being completely unconscious and fully conscious. This period generally lasts no more than a few seconds but it could be as much as half a minute or a minute. These "experienced dreams" are therefore pretty brief, and must be measured in seconds rather than minutes or hours.

DO PEOPLE DREAM IN COLOR?

Yes, most people have had dreams in color at some time or another but these tend to be the exception rather than the rule. The rule seems to be that the more use we make of color in our daily life, the more likely we are to dream in color. Women are more likely to dream in color than men, and creative people, particularly artists, are most likely to dream in color.

WHY IS IT SO DIFFICULT TO REMEMBER YOUR DREAMS?

Most dreams, as we have said, are not *experienced* and therefore cannot be remembered. The brain evidently keeps its sleeping and waking selves strictly separate—presumably to prevent confusion of their different memories. Thus even when sleep has been interrupted and a dream experienced, some mechanism comes into action which deliberately sets out to erase or repress the memory of the dream. Occasionally some event during the day will trigger the memory off but this does not happen too often. It would obviously be very inconvenient if one did remember too many dreams for in the course of time they would become confused with memories of "facts."

DO ANIMALS DREAM?

All high animals, and in particular warm-blooded ones, dream regularly and substantially. The amount of dreaming seems to be related to the general complexity of their brains and therefore it is not surprising to find that the animal who sleeps and dreams the most is man, with the other primates—chimpanzees, monkeys, etc.—not far behind. Next on the list come the carnivores—cats, dogs, lions, tigers, etc.—and rodents, whose lifestyles cause them to put their brains to constant use. Sheep and less intelligent animals sleep less, as do reptiles and fish. Very simple creatures such as insects, whose brains have little flexibility, find time for neither sleep nor dreams.

More about dreams

We have long been fascinated by the meaning of our dreams. But it is only comparatively recently that we have begun to understand them. We are now aware, for instance, that if we have a sexual dream about someone we hardly know, it could represent a forbidden love. And that men dream twice as much about other men as they do about women.

Dream interpretation can explain whole areas of your waking life and give meaning to recurring dreams which may puzzle you. To help you to understand your dreams, we present the second part of our "A to Z" guide to dream symbols. Once again we emphasize that the guide is not intended to give instant interpretation but only to indicate what certain symbols are thought to mean. This meaning is based on research into the dream life of men and women in many parts of the world.

In the early 1950s Calvin Hall, an American psychologist, studied 10,000 dreams and found some consistencies in the content. Since then he and his associate, R. L. Van de Castle, have continued their research on dream content. Most people move in their dreams, walk, run or ride—but we hardly ever carry out mundane chores like washing dishes. Dreamers travel, socialize and play, but rarely work. Passive, quiet activities are more common than strenuous ones.

If you are aged between 18 and 28, there is a 43 percent chance that a stranger figures in your dream. Older people tend to dream more of family members and less of strangers and friends. Why so many strangers? Probably they are people we know in disguise. A person who sees his father as a stern authority figure may transmute him into some other authority figure, a policeman, a teacher, a judge. A sexual dream about someone you know slightly and are not in reality attracted to could stand for a forbidden love. Most people commonly dream of people their own age—about 42 percent of the time. Children dream of their parents, parents of their children, and

Dream symbols have an otherworldly quality; even the most mundane objects and actions take on surreal dimensions.

Jim Burns

husbands and wives about each other.

Different patterns reveal themselves in the dreams of men and women. Women often find themselves indoors, in familiar settings; people appear more frequently, and are remembered in considerable detail; men and women figure in roughly equal numbers. As we might expect, rather fewer aggressive dreams are reported, and aggression tends to be verbal not physical. In the early months of pregnancy, women dream a great deal about their husbands, but in the last three months babies appear seven times more frequently.

Sometimes, too, labor is magically over and the baby has been born and is walking or even talking. Anxiety is shown by the dreams about babies weighing only ounces, or being giants of 35 pounds. Occasionally, women dream of giving birth to animals or a whole series of babies. The physiological changes of menstruation alter the character of women's dreams— the colors red and pink are more often noted (women tend to have more colored dreams than men in general), references to the human body increase, rooms within structures crop up. Social interactions change—men in a woman's dreams are much less friendly than at other times in her cycle.

Animals and Adventure

Hall and Castle found that men dream twice as much about men as they do about women. Their dreams are often concerned with their job; and success and failure and ambition dreams are common. On the whole men have relatively adventurous dreams, a lot of them featuring physical activities, e.g. mountain climbing, baseball and so on. Half of all their aggressive encounters involve physical violence—usually with unfamiliar males. Men report more overt sex dreams than women and their sexual partners are frequently unfamiliar women.

Male and female adults do not dream much about animals—of 4,000 adult dreams only 7.5 percent involved animals. But children do. Young children dream frequently of being frightened by animals and insects like jungle creatures, bears, alligators and spiders. Their parents dream occasionally of dogs, horses, cats and birds. As children grow older the percentage of their animal dreams decreases dramatically. This may be because as the child matures other more sophisticated dream symbols are available, to represent the threatening forces around him.

Now check the guide which follows and see if any of the symbols occur in your dreams. This may help you to explain away a dream that has been bothering you for some time or it may give you an insight into your experiences by day.

Dream symbols A-Z Part 2

LAKE
In Freudian terms water is rather literally equated to the waters of the uterus and such dreams therefore suggest an unconscious wish to retreat from life and return to the womb. Hence water may also refer to female sexuality and clearly here the context of the dream is tremendously important to its interpretation. In the case of a lake a sense of placidity is implied. Jung incidentally sees expanses of water as denoting the unconscious into which the dreamer is preparing to dip himself. Once again there is a suggestion of a desire to retreat from reality.

MONSTERS
In both Freudian and Jungian terms, monsters are seen as being the personification of the "baser" emotions of anger, fear and desire. When monsters feature in the nightmares of children they are presumed to indicate the child's growing awareness of these powerful and "antisocial" drives within him.

NAKEDNESS
Contrary to general belief this is not a sexual dream in the ordinary sense. The Freudian view is that a dream of nudity is a signal from the unconscious telling the dreamer that he should be more liberated in one way or another in his daily life. Classically the dreamer is often naked in a public place—and yet is not embarrassed. Both Freud and Jung agree that the unconscious is advising the dreamer that his "liberation" will not be unfavorably received.

OLD AGE
Freudian analysts often see dreams of old age in a rather direct way—a reminder from the unconscious of the inevitable process of aging which none of us can ignore. Jung takes a radically different view and sees the presence of an old person in a dream as being associated with a concept of wisdom. Any statements made (in dreams) by elderly people should therefore be taken very seriously and acted upon wherever possible!

PREGNANCY
A dream of being pregnant may have a number of different interpretations in traditional analytic terms and reminds one again of the importance of context and mood in assessing the portent of the dream. In the case of a childless couple the dream may be straightforward "wish fulfillment." Many young girls who do not wish to become pregnant however often experience this dream at about the time they begin to lead a sexually active love life. In such cases it may either be connected with anxiety or possibly guilt. More symbolic interpretations see pregnancy in dreams as implying the acquisition of knowledge and power.

QUEEN
Freudian and Jungian interpretations are basically similar. For Jung any mature or authoritative figure (see Old Age) stands for a source of wisdom. For Freud the queen specifically represents the mother, who to the child represents the source of stability and authority. Similarly kings, emperors, judges and other ritually significant figures stand for the father and his all-powerful authority.

RING
The ring, whether it is the stone circle of the ancient Druids or the gold band which symbolizes the traditionally unbreakable bonds of marriage, has long had enormous ritual significance. It is one of the most powerful images drawn from the collective unconscious described by Jung and when it figures in dreams is, without exception, considered to be a sign that an event of quite exceptional

The Mansell Collection

and essentially alien. From this he inferred that it represented the psychic world, foreign and potentially dangerous to human beings.

TEETH
Most dreams about teeth feature them cracking or falling out. A straightforward explanation which requires no symbolic interpretation is that the dreamer is suffering from mild toothache whose signals are disturbing sleep and being cast into the form of a dream. Freud, however, believed that the loss of teeth essentially denoted sexual impotence or the fear of it. For Jung the loss of teeth symbolized childbearing or the coming of adolescence.

UNIFORM
A uniform is a ritual and highly stylized form of clothing, the most positive indication, so to speak, that the individual is fully clothed. In psychoanalysis any dream featuring uniforms or elaborate costumes may be explained by the rule of "reversal." Here the clothing actually stands for nakedness and the dream is basically sexual in origin.

VASE
All containers of this type, including cups, bottles, pockets and so on, refer in Freudian theory to the female sex organs and are the counterpart to the classic male equivalents in which sticks, towers or snakes refer to the penis. Jungian theory takes a quite different view and sees any container, cave, tunnel, etc. as implying something hidden or secret. Thus the unconscious itself might also be indicated, though a secret anxiety or wish on the part of the dreamer is more likely implied.

WAVES
Many analysts see waves, particularly when stormy and large, as symbolizing sexual intercourse and the orgasm. To Jungians however waves represent a stirring of the unconscious which is symbolized by large expanses of water. Mood is tremendously important here again; if the tides or waves are gentle, the creative powers of the unconscious are at work, if strong and turbulent, then serious conflicts are indicated.

XMAS
The festive aspect of Christmas is only marginally helpful in interpretation here. For Freudians any highly decorated object such as a Christmas tree has strong sexual connotations. All forms of gifts and presents which may be associated with Christmas in the dream similarly refer to the granting of sexual "favors."

YACHT
While boats having a passive role in the dream are suggestive of female sexuality, yachts have a different connotation. Most frequently they represent the dreamer himself, plotting his course through life. While to some degree he is at the mercy of the wind, broadly speaking he is able to control his own progress and destination. Dreams of this kind imply great confidence and self-approval.

ZOO
Almost invariably visits to zoos in dreams are coupled with a sense of foreboding and anxiety. To most psychoanalysts a collection of animals, dangerous and at the same time eager to escape from their insubstantial prisons, symbolizes the torrent of animal desires and motives which eagerly await their moment to overwhelm the so-called civilized conscious self.

significance is taking place in the unconscious mind. Freudian analysts invest it with less universal significance but when it appears it is taken to imply a tie or bond.

SPIDER
For Freud the spider refers to that aspect of a mother's personality which is most unpleasant and terrifying to the child. At the root of the symbol is the notion that the spider/mother wishes to imprison her son so he can never get another woman of his own. Jung took a strikingly different view, seeing the spider as both cold-blooded

Marshall Cavendish

Sleep's mysteries

To sleep, perchance to . . . well, not just dream. All sorts of things are going on while we enjoy what Macbeth, quite rightly, called "the chief nourisher of life's feast." Sleep is so essential that, deprived of it, we would first become irritable and disorientated, then die.

About one-third of our lifetime is spent in sleep. But why is it necessary? What does it do for us? In general, this still remains largely a mystery, although we are now in a position to make some suggestions.

Historically there have always been great difficulties in the study of sleep. There are limits to the amount of information that can be obtained by direct observation of people asleep, while the trouble with questionnaires is that people can remember little of their experience during sleep.

The recent growth in research on the subject is due to the discovery of an effective new tool for observing brain processes during sleep—the electroencephalogram, known colloquially as EEG. This is a machine which records the electrical activity in the brain, known as brain waves.

Two Kinds of Sleep

When a man is awake his brain waves show a fairly regular rhythm of about ten cycles per second. This is the alpha rhythm. As he falls asleep the brain waves become progressively slower and less regular—he is now in the state called **orthodox sleep**. After about an hour, however, the brain waves begin to show a more active pattern again, even though the person is apparently asleep very deeply. This is called **paradoxical sleep** because it has much in common with being awake.

During orthodox (or passive) sleep the brain is apparently resting; its blood supply is reduced and its temperature falls slightly. Breathing and heart rate are regular. The muscles, however, remain slightly tensed. Paradoxical (or active) sleep is marked by irregular breathing and heart rate, increased blood supply to the brain and increased brain temperature. Most of the muscles are relaxed. There are various jerky movements of the body and face, including short bursts of rapid eye movement (REMs) which occur behind the closed eyelids.

Sweet Dreams, Sweet Temper

Orthodox sleep is broken up by about five periods of paradoxical sleep which are of progressively longer duration throughout the course of the night. Overall, about one-quarter of our sleep is of the paradoxical kind. Interestingly, the proportion of sleep that is paradoxical is greatest in the newborn child (constituting more than half the total sleep duration); it decreases with age, most steeply in the first few weeks after birth, and again in senility. It is generally very low in mentally defective persons.

Paradoxical sleep seems to be a higher evolutionary form: it does not occur in reptiles; appears only very briefly in birds; but is strongly evident in mammals, particularly the newborn of the species.

Clearly, in studying sleep we are dealing with two completely different phenomena. It is not simply a matter of going to sleep at night and waking up again in the morning—we spend the night alternating between two different types of sleep, so different

in fact that we can probably expect them to have different brain mechanisms and different purposes.

There is a theory that we spend part of the night working on the brain (paradoxical sleep) and the rest of the night working on the rest of the body (orthodox sleep). Presumably these two restoration jobs would be taken in turns so that at whatever time it is necessary for us to wake we will have received some benefit from each of them. This is almost certainly an oversimplification but there is some evidence that fits quite neatly. For example, it has been shown that athletes, whose life style presumably puts a great deal of strain on their bodies, need more orthodox sleep. Children need a greater amount of both kinds of sleep to allow for growth, and especially paradoxical sleep in the early weeks when the gray matter of the brain is developing very quickly.

What happens if we are prevented from sleeping? Initially, nothing very much. But our performance soon begins to deteriorate, particularly on tasks that require sustained concentration. As sleeplessness progresses, behavior becomes more and more disorganized, while the person becomes incoherent and irritable. After a few days without sleep he is likely to have delusions and hallucinations. Further deprivation of sleep would probably lead to full-blown psychosis and eventually death. The biological necessity of sleep is unquestionable.

Some researchers deprived their volunteers of paradoxical sleep only, permitting them the usual amount of orthodox sleep but waking them every time the EEG indicated that a period of paradoxical sleep was beginning. Such selective sleep deprivation resulted in a kind of "rebound effect"—the amount of paradoxical sleep was subsequently increased relative to orthodox, apparently in order to make up for what was lost.

Sleep, Nature's Restorer

The typical human sleeping pattern is based on a 24 hour cycle and averages at about 8 hours, say between 11 p.m. and 7 a.m. This is slightly determined by biological factors, but unlike the menstrual cycle in women, the timing of it appears to have been established largely by habit. It is convenient for us to sleep at night and work during the daylight hours when we can see what we are doing.

How about people who work night shifts, like doctors, nurses and watchmen? Are they able to perform their work with equal proficiency? Yes, provided they are used to it. But if they have acquired a normal night-sleep pattern and are asked to work through odd nights, then their level of competence will almost certainly be below par.

It is widely believed that sleep has a restorative function, both psychologically and physically. According to Macbeth it is "sore labor's bath, balm of hurt minds, great nature's second

Right: Most of us can sleep through quite loud noise. This is because we have been "switched off" by a control center in the brain. When you hear a sound while awake (top), the Reticular Activating System alerts the brain. In light sleep (also known as orthodox or passive sleep), the Raphe System, in a part of the brain stem called the pons (bottom left), secretes serotonin, a hormone. This switches off the fast cortex wave (which makes the brain active) and eye movement. Muscle tone is left "on." In deep dream sleep (paradoxical or active sleep), another system in the pons, the locus coeruleus (bottom right), sends out the hormone noradrenalin which cancels the effects of serotonin. Noradrenalin cuts muscle tone signals off while switching on eye movement and the fast cortex wave. During this time the brain is restored. Left: It is deep dream or paradoxical sleep we need most when we are young and growing and less as we grow older (see chart).

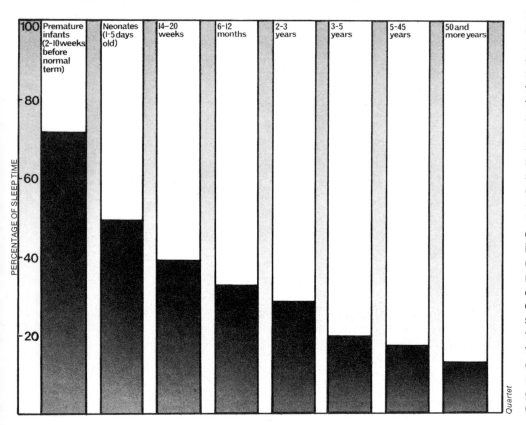

PERCENTAGE OF SLEEP TIME

| 100 | Premature infants (2-10 weeks before normal term) | Neonates (1-5 days old) | 14–20 weeks | 6-12 months | 2-3 years | 3-5 years | 5-45 years | 50 and more years |

Quartet

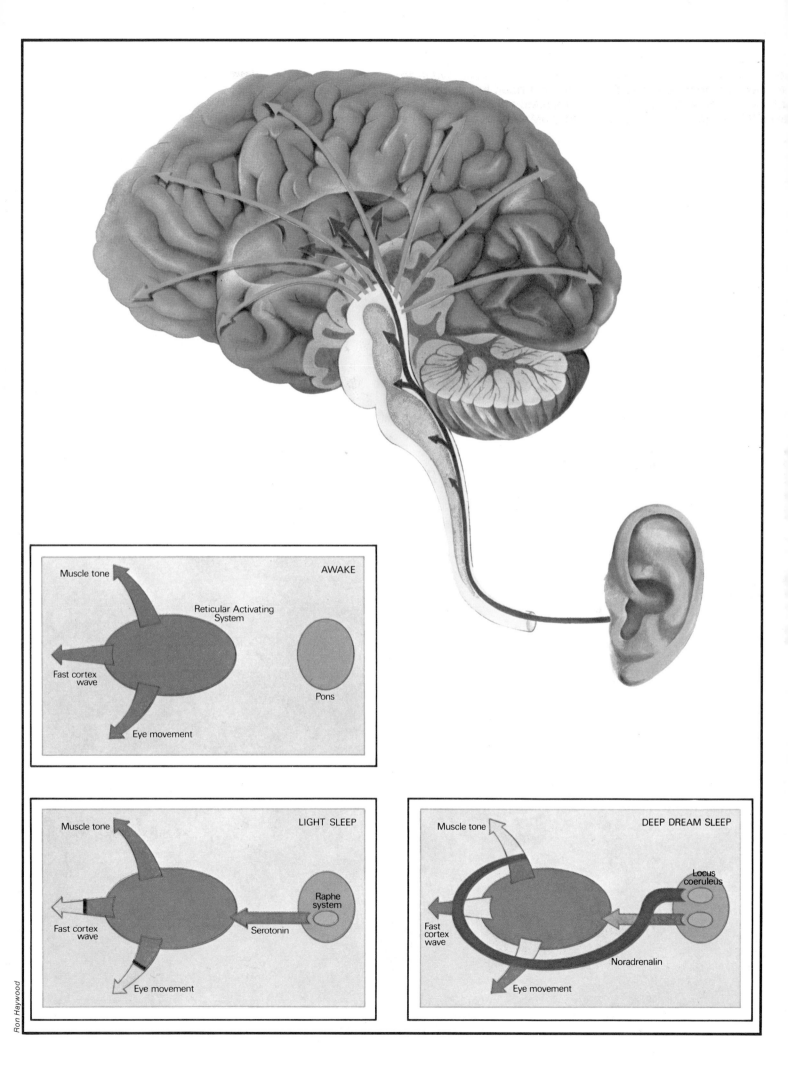

Muscle tone

AWAKE

Reticular Activating
System

Fast cortex
wave

Pons

Eye movement

Muscle tone

LIGHT SLEEP

Fast cortex
wave

Raphe
system

Serotonin

Eye movement

Muscle tone

DEEP DREAM SLEEP

Locus
coeruleus

Fast
cortex
wave

Noradrenalin

Eye movement

Ron Haywood

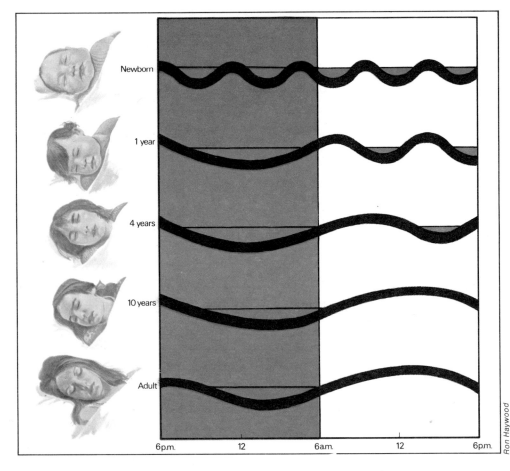

Ron Haywood

6 p.m.　12　6 a.m.　12　6 p.m.

Sleep patterns. The red areas indicate sleep, the peaked black line wakefulness. A baby sleeps fitfully by night and day. Between the ages of one and four the child has a longer night sleep and naps by day. By age ten only a night sleep is necessary. Then normal adult sleep becomes fixed.

course, chief nourisher in life's feast." The truth in this popular notion seems undeniable, but what precisely is being restored during sleep? Presumably the cells that make up our body. They are not static: they increase in numbers by a process of division, especially in our early years, and they are replaced when damaged. Sleep probably facilitates the processes of cell growth and the regeneration of bodily functions.

Recharging the Batteries

To some extent, this might also occur while we are awake, but ideally it requires a redirection of our energy resources away from the organs involved in waking activity. Thus most of the body's machinery shuts down for the night in order to conserve enough energy for cell growth and regeneration. Like recharging the batteries of an electric car, it does not matter exactly when it is done provided it occurs with some regularity —otherwise performance becomes progressively slow and unreliable.

Even though we now know something about the mysteries of sleep, we are still a long way from understanding it completely. Great strides have been made in understanding the "what," "when" and "how," but "why" remains one of the most veiled mysteries of sleep and brain functions in general.

HOW MUCH SLEEP DO YOU NEED?

A reasonable average is eight hours a night but anything between six and ten is normal. Ten might be a little on the long side, only because it cuts rather a lot into the day. Some healthy people can get by on as little as five and, at a stretch, four hours' sleep, but these are exceptions. The main thing is that there is no hard and fast rule and the real question to ask yourself is how *you* feel after your average night's sleep.

WHY DO WE SLEEP LESS AS WE GET OLDER?

As one gets older one tends to do, on the whole, fewer and fewer "new" things and the sleep process of filing and reorganizing becomes less and less significant and fewer and fewer hours need to be set aside for this purpose. Thus as we get older so our sleep requirement falls off.

IS IT POSSIBLE TO DO WITHOUT SLEEP ALTOGETHER?

The answer is definitely no. Many people claim not to sleep at all but when investigated by scientists it has been found that they do fall asleep though they are not aware of it! Some people, for psychological reasons, may go through periods of having immense difficulty sleeping and after a period of intense shock, such as the loss of a close relative, may be unable

to sleep for two or three nights in a row. Sooner or later the sleep drive overcomes them however and their cycle returns gradually to normal.

IS IT POSSIBLE TO HAVE TOO MUCH SLEEP?

For the normal healthy person the answer is no—one will sleep just as much as one's brain requires. Very heavy and excessive sleep—say over ten hours at a stretch—if it occurs frequently is often a sign of depression and in some cases may denote a physical illness of some kind. There are some illnesses of a tropical origin in which people sleep more or less perpetually.

CAN YOU PAY OFF A SLEEP DEBT WITH AN EXTRA LONG NIGHT'S SLEEP?

It depends on how great is the sleep debt, but if one is talking about just missing one or possibly two nights' sleep, then a single really good night's rest will get rid of the backlog. Sometimes more than one night is required. People who have been under immense strain—say the survivors of some major accident or disaster—may sleep for 24 or 36 hours at a stretch.

CAN YOU LEARN WHEN YOU ARE ASLEEP?

Recent research has shown that the brain is highly active throughout sleep and is performing all kinds of operations vital to its survival. For this reason, even if you could feed in information during sleep, the results might be more harmful than beneficial. As it happens, the experimental evidence that we can learn when we sleep is very thin. Experiments which claim to show that sleeping subjects had absorbed information fed to them through a pillow speaker have been discounted by most scientists, because the experimenters have not taken sufficient precautions to ensure that their subjects really were asleep. When the experiments were repeated while the subjects' brainwaves were monitored to determine whether they were sleeping or not, and information was only fed in when the brain waves indicated sleep, no evidence of sleep learning was found.

Marshall Cavendish

Sexual attraction

You know the feeling. But do you know that the body has a "language" all of its own; a signaling system that says "You excite me"? It's a fact that two people can "speak" to each other without saying a word.

The joys, pleasures, agonies and ecstasies of sexual attraction have for centuries been the topic of poets and philosophers, playwrights, painters and, of course, pornographers.

The flicker of mutual attraction between a couple meeting for the first time "across a crowded room," the ardent pursuit of the seducer, the more stable relationship of adult love,

the erotic fantasies of wishful dreamers are all expressions of a sexual drive common to our species.

Indeed, sex, in terms of procreation as opposed to recreation, is essential to our survival; and in that respect we share, with much of the animal kingdom, a behavior pattern designed initially to attract male and female, second to engender a state of increas-

ing intimacy, and finally to bring about copulation.

This may not sound too romantic, or even enchanting, and hardly the stuff that Shakespeare's Romeo and Juliet were made of; but balconies are not essential prerequisites to sexual gymnastics though they may be a handy prop for poets.

Our immediate concern here is not

with magic, black, white or otherwise, but with the highly sophisticated and no less intriguing ways in which we, like many animals, employ techniques to arouse physically a member of the opposite sex—techniques whose ultimate purpose is the *natural* objective of sexual intercourse, whatever the actual intentions of the couple.

Scientific experiments have demonstrated that when two people are sexually attracted physiological changes occur as the body gears itself for the encounter; and these changes, like the more overt behavior patterns that accompany them, are largely automatic.

Take a pair of strangers at a party. He, on his way to get a drink, suddenly notices her. He does not know her, has not spoken to her, but cannot stop glancing at her. He is sexually attracted to her.

At this point he is unaware that his pulse rate, which normally stands at 70-80 per minute, has increased to around 90; that his blood pressure has increased and that he, is breathing more rapidly. Imperceptibly, he has tensed his muscles and is standing in a more erect posture. Should someone speak to him now he will probably be startled and not so easily able to make natural conversation as he is distracted and slightly "agitated."

She, from the other side of the room, returns one of his glances with a slight smile and with that a two-way communication has tentatively begun. Their behavior thereafter follows an exploratory pattern in sexual communication which is amazingly direct yet carried on without the aid of real verbal communication.

Pair Formation

Desmond Morris, the well-known zoologist, describes three phases of sexual behavior in our species: pair formation, precopulatory activity and copulation. The pair formation stage, usually referred to as courtship (though not necessarily in the old-fashioned sense of preparation for marriage), is remarkably prolonged by animal standards, frequently lasting for weeks or months. It is the stage our imaginary couple are about to embark on.

As with many other species there is a tentative ambivalent behavior involving fear, aggression and sexual attraction. The nervousness and hesitancy is slowly reduced if the subsequent behavior pattern—the mutual sexual signals—is strong enough. So what *are* the sexual signals involved and how do we interpret them?

He, when he first saw her, involuntarily tightened his muscles and stood more erect. When she returned his glance she blushed—or at least looked more "flushed," and this was because her arteries and veins had dilated to allow a greater flow of blood from the deeper regions to the surface areas of the body.

This "sexual glow" is most commonly seen in the female and is more obvious during intense sexual arousal. In both instances, however, our couple were unwittingly increasing their physical attractiveness.

Albert Scheflen of Bronx State Hospital in New York has drawn attention to items of "agitated" behavior, which, he suggests, might be doing precisely the same thing. When a woman touches her face, pushes her hair back or adjusts her clothes she is enhancing her own attractiveness and drawing the other's attention. Similarly, a man may adjust his tie or jacket or comb his hair. Scheflen calls this preening behavior and proposes that it occurs as a direct result of one individual's attraction for another. There are obvious parallels in animal life—the ruff bird who displays his intricate collar or the cob from Uganda his glorious throat for his intended's delight.

Eye Contact

By far the most powerful signal in sexual attraction is the face and particularly the eyes. The face is, without doubt, the most expressive region in the entire body. Through it we reveal the entire range of human emotion. As a device for inviting intimacy it is of major importance. A face that is soft, relaxed and smiling or one that is alert and excited in response to our physical presence obviously finds us attractive.

It is the eyes, however, that *see* such signals as the smile and it is the eyes that transmit on their own the most powerful sexual signals.

Of course we all need to look at people with whom we are talking in order to learn their reaction, to check their changing moods. If, however, we continue to gaze or stare at another for a prolonged time we are engaging in intimate behavior.

Initially, our couple probably held their glance a little longer than is usual, thereby testing each other but at the same time hinting at the desire for further contact. If they continue to gaze at each other, thereby indicating mutual feelings of attraction, they are engaging in what is called eye contact. The prolonged gaze is not,

of course, the only form of eye contact. The wink may be interpreted as a direct invitation to sexual intercourse. The demure dropping of the eyes also transmits its message in the female as does fluttering of the eyelashes.

Another fascinating eye signal is pupillary dilation. Under the influence of strong emotions of a pleasant kind the pupil (the small dark spot in the center of the eye) grows much larger. Centuries before it was ever studied scientifically Italian beauties were known to create the effect artificially with belladonna and Chinese jade dealers used this response as a means of assessing the degree of interest shown by customers.

In a study by the American psychologist Eckhard Hess, a group of men were shown two apparently identical photographs of the same girl. One, in fact, had been retouched so that the girl's pupils were enlarged and it was this one that the men preferred, found more attractive, although they were unable to say why.

Yet another eye change occurs under intense emotion and that is a small increase in tear production. Weeping with joy is not a common occurrence but the obvious glistening shiny eyes of lovers are a by-product of this physiological change.

Because eye contact is so directly linked with sexual intimacy there is a strong social taboo prohibiting it among strangers. Most of us have experienced embarrassment and sometimes outrage at being stared at in public places or when in a bus or train. When two strangers do accidentally find that their eyes meet they quickly avert their gaze or find something else to look at. Reading a newspaper in a crowded bus or train provides the perfect defense against the discomfort of eye contact.

Bodily Contact and Touching

In Western culture there is, likewise, a taboo on touching strangers. If we brush against a stranger in a crowded street, one or the other of us usually apologizes, we lower our eyes and hurry away. Bodily contact is only permissible in certain circumstances. We shake hands as a formal greeting; we may kiss an acquaintance of either sex affectionately on both cheeks; on the dance floor we permit embraces which in other circumstances we would consider highly intimate.

In the initial stages of sexual attraction touching behavior remains within conventional boundaries but at the same time subtle signals are trans-

Marshall Cavendish

mitted and received. Perhaps the handshake contains an almost imperceptible caressing of the fingers; she may touch his hand as he lights her cigarette or thread her arm through his as they walk from the dance floor. As the relationship develops touching increases and the parts of the body accessible to the partner's touch become more numerous.

Linked with touching is another signal which we will call orientation. This refers to the angle in which people position themselves when talking. Among strangers this is usually at an angle so that they can look at each other yet at the same time keep an eye on what is happening around them and, when desired, more easily move away.

Attraction is, as often as not, signaled when a couple directly face each other. It shows exclusive interest in each other and this way they can more easily make eye contact. As the relationship progresses they may move to a side-by-side position because this allows greater bodily contact.

Space between People

Important, also, is the distance which people observe between each other. The American anthropologist Edward Hall suggests that there are distinct zones which people adhere to —the intimate zone (0-18 inches); personal distance (18 inches-4 feet); social-consultative distance (4-10 feet); and public distance (10 feet upwards). When sexual attraction exists between a couple they adopt a distance at the closer end of the zone range for a particular situation.

At their party our couple would have tended to stand about 18-20 inches apart, thereby positioning themselves at the closer end of the personal distance zone. Had they met at a business meeting they would have signaled their mutual attraction by standing only 4 feet apart. In this area, however, cultural differences occur and to the unaware the signals can get misinterpreted. The normal distance for conversation is much closer in Southern European countries than in the United States and Northern Europe.

Consequently, an English woman may feel discomfort in Italy where, in fact, closer distances are perfectly normal because she misreads the

In the later stages of their relationship lovers cannot resist engaging in frequent body-to-body and face-to-face contact.

Blushing and an increase in the size of the pupils are unconscious forms of communication: in the woman on the right they indicate strong interest, and also make her seem more attractive. Throughout the ages women have used cosmetics to create this effect artificially. Similarly, advertizers touch up photographs of model girls, to make them more appealing. Pupil size has been studied in the laboratory with interesting results — women's pupils grow big seeing the picture of a baby; men's enlarge for a nude woman.

Distance and the angle at which people stand at parties were studied by Australian scientist Glen McBride. He observed that people stand roughly at 45 degree angles to each other and constantly adjust their position to retain that angle. Interestingly, McBride found the same arrangements among hens in a fairly crowded chicken yard. When a couple break this convention by standing face to face it allows them to engage in eye contact and indicates their exclusive interest in each other.

distance as a kind of sexual signal. This can and does lead to serious misunderstandings because we feel that a taboo has been violated.

Tone of Voice and Speech

Perhaps the least important of signals in sexual attraction is the one which distinguishes us most from the animal kingdom—speech. Indeed, we often find it very difficult to make "intelligent" conversation in the initial stages of attraction and find ourselves stuttering and hesitant. Speech can thus interfere with the effectiveness of body language, although at a later stage when nervousness is reduced it can lend credibility to our nonverbal signals.

Of vital importance, however, is tone of voice. A courting couple is often referred to as "murmuring sweet nothings" and this phrase sums up neatly the significance of the tone of voice as opposed to what is being spoken.

Male and Female Differences in Dealing with Sexual Attraction

In our society, at least, it is traditional for the male to be the initiator of sexual approaches, although some women would like it otherwise. This is indirectly supported by a New York newspaper, *The Village Voice,* which conducted a survey on women's views of male attractiveness. They revealed that the women questioned thought it somewhat irregular to be asked to view men as sex objects.

When pressed they *did* give their views, but it is the male, still, who, by and large, sees a "sex object" and the female who responds according to the customs of her society.

By looking at a woman whom he finds attractive a man is, in effect, putting a proposition to her. She can respond by either returning his gaze, thereby signaling she is not averse to further contact, or looking away and thus rejecting his advance. The same approach-response sequence will operate with other forms of sexual signals.

The intense emotions communicated through nonverbal signals can either be satisfied once and for all in sexual intercourse or they can be the basis for an ongoing sexual and emotional involvement of a less dramatic kind. This, however, brings us to the complex question of what and who is attractive to us? What attracts us sexually and why we sometimes seemingly inexplicably choose the partner we do are intriguing subjects in themselves.

Touching is an invitation to intimacy, but at first it is likely to be disguised as politeness or good manners. Holding a woman's arm or hand to help her cross a street, clutching her arm as support if she slips or trips, guiding her through a crowded room are examples. Such disguises are necessary at this stage so that either party can reject or accept the invitation without embarrassment, since such behavior is socially acceptable. The woman can thank the man and leave, or respond with a gesture of encouragement. Only when they are confident in their mutual attraction does touching and hand holding increase. It is then no longer a supporting or guiding act but undisguised intimacy.

Elizabeth Moyes

Sigmund Freud Copyrights Ltd.

Freud and sexuality

Freud shocked the world and the shock waves still echo today. What did he *really* say about man's sexuality?

Ask anyone to name a famous psychologist. Almost certainly he will say Sigmund Freud; for more than any other thinker of the late nineteenth and early twentieth century Freud set his stamp on modern civilization and modern thinking.

Freud's name is inevitably associated with "sex"—a taboo subject in the Victorian era. "People believed him a crazy man who saw sex in everything. Ladies blushed when you mentioned his name," said Max Graf, a former student of Freud's. Indeed, when his name cropped up at a neurological conference in 1910 an outraged German professor exclaimed, "This is not a topic for discussion at a scientific meeting; it is a matter for the police!" But what *were* Freud's theories about sexuality and why did they so enrage the Victorian world?

Freud found that his patients revealed urges and feelings of a sexual nature and, even more, they produced memories which showed that even in childhood their sexual urges were wild consuming passions. As a result he decided that repressed sexual feelings were at the root of all mental illness, and that even among normally adjusted people sexuality played a predominant part in the functioning of the mind. This was pretty inflammatory stuff and when it was this aspect of his work that he most emphasized, it was hardly surprising that his opponents reacted with horror and fury. Curiously, the fury was even less than it might have been. Most people had not read his work because the greater part of it was simply unprintable.

What Freud Really Said

According to Freud, sexual life does not begin only at puberty but starts with clear manifestations soon after birth. Freud, indeed, to the outrage of Victorian morality, described the infant as a polymorphous pervert. But sexual life for Freud has a meaning different from that usually given it. "Sexual life comprises the function of obtaining pleasure from zones of the body—a function which is subsequently brought into the service of that of reproduction," to quote Freud's actual words. From this it is clear that, in the Freudian view, all kinds of sensual pleasure, from any part of the body, are a part of sexuality. Sexuality, then, is far wider than the mature, adult sexual desire.

In the first year of life this infant sexuality manifests itself through the mouth which is the center of pleasurable excitation. This is the *oral phase* and this sexual drive is known as *oral eroticism*. The oral phase itself divides into two stages, first the oral erotic where the pleasure involves sucking, then the oral sadistic when biting becomes important. This is the Freudian explanation, in part, of what all

Sigmund Freud Copyrights Ltd.

3

4

1. Freud aged ten, with his father, Jakob. Sigmund later realized he had been deeply jealous of Jakob's relationship with his beloved mother. 2. Amalia Freud with her eldest son, Sigmund. He remained her undisputed favorite. 3. Freud married Martha Bernays in 1886 after a four-year engagement. Their happy marriage lasted 53 years. 4. Portrait of Freud aged 64. By 1920 his theories were just beginning to find wide attention and acceptance.

mothers know only too well, the tendency for everything to go into the mouth regardless of suitability and the painful phase of oral sadism for those who are breast feeding.

About the third year the anus becomes the chief center of excitation— the erotogenic zone. This is the *anal phase.* Here, according to Freud, the child gets pleasure from expelling his feces, at the first part of the anal stage, and later from retaining his feces. It should be noted that the anal phase is often coincident with the time of toilet training.

At about four years of age begins the *phallic stage.* Here the chief erotogenic zone is the penis for the boy and for the girl the clitoris. This is still different from adult sexuality in that the pleasure derived from these sexual organs is divorced from ideas of sexual intercourse; boys for instance become interested in the size of their penises and in the power of their urination.

After this phallic stage at around five years of age the Oedipus complex and castration complex contrive to repress infantile sexuality until at puberty the final phase, the *genital phase*, of sexual organization is established. At this stage all the previous phases are organized and subordinated to the adult sexual aim of pleasure in the reproductive function. It will not have escaped most readers that mature sexual behavior, especially as advised in love manuals, involves oral, anal and phallic eroticism.

The Psychological Importance of the Theory

If Freudian psychosexual theory stated merely that children obtained sexual pleasure from different parts of the body at different ages, it would be interesting but trivial. However, this infantile sexuality is crucial to the whole personality development of the child. This is because it cannot always be directly expressed, but may have to be repressed or sublimated. Freud, indeed, said that "permanent character traits are either unchanging perpetuations of the original impulse (pregenital eroticism), sublimations of them or reaction formations against

them." Some examples will make this more clear.

Thus, in Freudian theory, unchanging perpetuations of oral eroticism would include a fondness for deep kissing, compared with other sexual caresses, a strong interest in eating and drinking, addiction to smoking or chewing gum. In Western society oral eroticism can be directly expressed. Anal eroticism, however, has almost no overt expression other than in sexual perversions such as sodomy which still arouses much emotion, as demonstrated by the film *Last Tango in Paris.* One of the few direct expressions of anal eroticism is the excessive interest in bowel movements cleverly exploited by drug manufacturers.

Now if infantile sexuality cannot be expressed it is sublimated or there are reaction formations against it. Sublimation usually involves a deflection of aim. Thus in Freudian theory the sublimation of the desire to handle feces is the desire to handle paint. Thus artists are sublimating their anal eroticism. Sublimation of the desire to retain feces becomes parsimony: the retention of fecal symbols—money. Reaction formation involves creating the opposite attitude to the impulse. Thus the desire to smear feces becomes cleanliness.

Since anal eroticism has little direct expression in our culture but is almost entirely sublimated or reacted against, Freud postulated that this

was the origin of a collection of personality traits which he found quite frequently together in his patients—orderliness, obstinacy and parsimony. From its childhood origin he named it the anal character. Thus we can see how expression and sublimations of our infant sexuality produce our character traits and attitudes.

Your Son, Your Rival

Freud believed that infantile sexuality culminated in the Oedipus and castration complexes. Around the age of five a boy "desires to possess [his mother] physically in the ways in which he has divined from his observations and intuitive surmises of sexual life . . . his father now becomes a rival who stands in his way and whom he would like to push aside." The Oedipal period finally comes to an end when the boy, fearing the father may punish him with castration for his illicit desires for his mother accepts the reality of the situation, begins to identify with his father and to develop a conscience (the super ego).

Freud also advanced the notion that girls become jealous of the apparent genital superiority of boys ("penis envy") and so turn against their mother whom they hold responsible for their lack and towards their father. This is the Electra complex. When girls begin to identify with their mother there is an end to these feelings. Thus the Oedipus and Electra complexes mean that children love the opposite sex parent and hate the other. Identification with the hated parent brings an end to these feelings and the child enters a sexually quiescent period, which goes on until puberty.

The impact of such theories is today still shocking if we think of them applying *personally* to our own family. Is Freudian theory too fantastic and far-fetched? Perhaps. But examples of the Oedipus and castration complex abound everywhere. The man who cannot marry because no woman can equal his mother, the man who can have sexual relations only with women he despises, the man whose choice of spouse is determined by similarity or dissimilarity with his mother, the man who cannot submit to any authority—all exemplify failure to deal successfully with these complexes. In theory, too, the single woman who devotes her life to her mother demonstrates a reaction formation against Oedipal jealousy.

How Sexy was Freud?

Freud's private life was very separate from the public scandals he caused. He may well have based his theory of the Oedipus complex on his own relationship with his parents—he was his mother's favorite son and she played an important part in his life, right through her indomitable old age. He was certainly a passionate young man. In April 1882 he met Martha Bernays, the sister of his friend Eli, and fell in love with her immediately. For three weeks, he struggled with his feelings; he was a poor student, in no position even to think of marriage (and he seems never to have thought of any other relationship with her); but his feelings were too strong to be dismissed. He courted her ardently, idealized her beyond the bounds of reality, suffered torments of jealousy. On June 17, two months after they met, they became secretly engaged; Martha's mother disapproved of him, and was in the habit of removing her daughter to Hamburg to try

Freud said, "Sexual life comprises the function of obtaining pleasure from zones of the body"—a daring statement for that era. Whatever the prevailing attitudes it was indisputable that there are erogenous zones—shaded in the illustration—from which pleasure is derived.

to break up their attachment—not that he had yet formed his startling theories, but he was poor and not sufficiently orthodox in religion. During their separations, he had to write to her secretly, using the man he feared as his rival as an intermediary. Later, he was to claim that women are more jealous than men. Perhaps he had forgotten his early letters, demanding, accusing, agonizing. Martha loved him but, being a gentle and sweet-tempered girl, could not hurt her family by refusing to accompany her mother. She gave him a picture of herself, hidden in a box; as he studied, Freud would take it out constantly to urge him on, so that they could marry when he could provide a home. When he went to study surgery at the General Hospital in Vienna, he wrote, "I will not leave you to anyone . . . no one else's love compares with mine."

The next four years were spent in feverish impatience, together with the realization that love was not enough. "What is our dowry?" he wrote. "Nothing but love for each other. Nothing else? Now it occurs to me that we would need two or three little rooms to live and eat in and to receive a guest, and a stove in which the fire for our meals never goes out. And just think of all the things that have to go into the rooms! Tables and chairs, beds, mirrors, a clock to remind the happy couple of the passage of time, an armchair for an hour's pleasant daydreaming . . ." He ended this long letter, ". . . without you I would let my arms droop for sheer lack of desire to live; with you, for you, I will make use of them to gain our share in this world so as to enjoy it with you."

Family Life

They were at last married on September 13, 1886. With Martha safely his, his jealousy and romantic frustration died away. Theirs was a good marriage, for life. We do not know how Freud fared as a lover, but they had six children in the first ten years of their marriage.

Though he himself hinted that it ceased to be important in their marriage, the sex life of the man who changed the meaning of sex was moral, loving and monogamous. In 1936, the Freuds celebrated their Golden Wedding Anniversary, and Freud affectionately said that life with Martha "was really not a bad solution of the marriage problem."

Carol Binch

B.F.I.

Territory and defense

Why do you get angry when someone parks outside your door? Many scientists would say that getting and protecting territory is one of man's most basic urges.

Our instinctive defense of territory arises in many different situations. One of the most obvious is the attitude we take towards our car. In a recent court case in Germany the judge ruled that the defendant, who had killed a man for sneering at his Mercedes, had committed an act of justifiable homicide. He was acquitted of the murder charge and released. The incident is clearly extreme but equally on a more standard level the tiniest bump is often enough to make car owners square up threateningly to each other, even if they do not resort to violence.

The Mercedes owner's case may seem absurd, although it should be remembered that most courts recognize the fundamental right of man to defend his territory even if it means killing an intruder. In a widely covered case some years ago a Mr. Marsden-

Smedley was threatened by a man in the course of business negotiations. When that man walked into his house for the final confrontation, Smedley shot him. At the trial he was judged to have acted within his legal right and consequently exonerated. This is another extreme incident, but again, on the more common level, haven't we all experienced anger and resentment when someone parks outside our house, when we are forced to share a table at a restaurant, or when someone sits at our office desk?

The Fight for Land

Only recently has this urge to defend one's territory, which has long been recognized and accepted in law, attracted the attention of scientists. For many years man was considered to be the only creature on earth in-

fluenced by territorial notions, but the idea that man was unique in this sense was discredited as a result of Henry Howard's study of the habits of birds published in 1920. Later work has supported his initial hypothesis that many species have a distinct feeling of territory which is inherent in their genetic behavior. According to Robert Ardrey, the competition between males that was formerly believed to be for the possession of females is in fact a struggle for the possession of land. Equally, where man is concerned, the Freudian notion of sex as the basis for all our behavior has now been eroded by mounting evidence that our drive is really aimed at gaining and defending an exclusive property. For in disputes over boundaries, rights of way, the straying of animals, or even retrieval of lost tennis balls, men often act with irrational aggression. This is expressed either overtly by abuse or ritualistically by lawyer's letters and expensive litigation. Whether as individuals, families, races or nations, men persistently defend their territories against intruders.

Territorial Boundaries

Cars, houses and countries form obvious physical territory, but studies of more subtle human boundaries have given us an increasingly fascinating picture of our instinctive behavior. Glen McBride, a lecturer in animal behavior in Australia, studied the habits of guests at cocktail parties and was struck by the manner in which people pose themselves in a crowded room. He discovered that people in conversation rarely face each other directly at close distance unless they are a male and female between whom there is a sexual attraction. Surely many of us can remember being forced to back away from an aggressive speaker who thrusts his face too close for comfort. However, if we sit side-by-side, in whatever discomfort, we are able to speak freely and lose our self-consciousness. Similarly if we stand in a crowded room we tend to adjust our bodies to stand at approximately 45 degrees to each other. On photographing hens in a fairly crowded

yard, McBride found the same response present when the chickens pecked together over the same pan. If one bird shifted the other would alter his angle appropriately to maintain 45 degrees. Only the highly dominant hens would move in to face another bird directly like the belligerent guest at a party.

From these observations McBride developed his concept of personal space. He suggests that surrounding us all is a "portable territory," the larger part of which lies to our front, in which we resent any intrusion. This space varies with sex, men requiring more, women less, a man and a woman together perhaps none at all. The space also varies with rank for if a well-known personality has a drink in a bar he will be talked to by an admiring circle who keep their distance. This kind of personal territory extends far beyond fences and doors, reaching jobs, departments, labor unions and even crime where the Mafia can fight over disputed areas of control. Similarly the robin will attack any intruder in his part of the garden.

Wearing dark glasses is a further symptom of the desire to create adequate personal space. They provide a darkened wall from behind which one can observe while preserving a degree of remoteness. Even now research is being carried out on the

relation of this social space to the mentally ill. A. H. Esser, an American psychiatrist, has discovered that mentally retarded children almost always establish fixed territories. Within those areas that the child regards as "his," his aggressive behavior drops by half, while even the most retarded child is able to learn when reassured by being in a "home" location. A further experiment with prisoners re-

For man or animals, territory is something vital to hold and defend. cob or antelope, like man, live within fixed but complex territorial limits. In the diagram below a medium-sized herd of cob scattered unevenly over the plains are actually in orderly territories based upon harmless aggressive displays and fights between bucks. A herd of cob is made up of several groups and some solitary animals, grazing or resting and chewing the cud. A few will be moving about restlessly, but never straying over an invisible boundary line enclosing the territory of the herd. Males display at each other across the boundaries of territories and usually have a harem of does within their own territories.

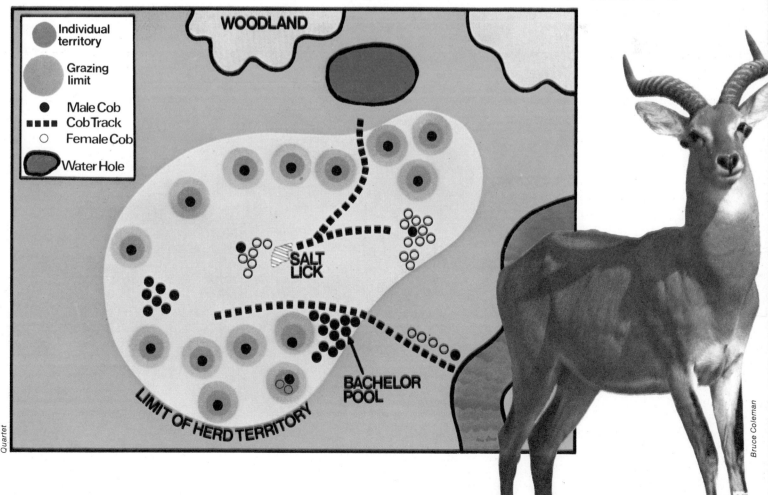

WOODLAND

- Individual territory
- Grazing limit
- Male Cob
- Cob Track
- Female Cob
- Water Hole

SALT LICK

BACHELOR POOL

LIMIT OF HERD TERRITORY

Quartet

Bruce Coleman

vealed that the least violent required four times less space than the most violent whose personal space did not extend to the front, but rather to the rear. Moreover, as confidence in the experimenter grew the demand for space dropped—and most dramatically in the rear projecting violent types.

So where does this urge for "space and territory" stem from? Are there biological reasons for it, and for the apparently "instinctual" aggression that infringement of territory appears to provoke? If man is a territorial creature we may gain a clue to his behavior from studies of other territorial species. For we know that in some animals aggressive behavior is inherently linked to occupation and defense of "property."

Aggressive Behavior in Animals

Ritual fighting in animals appears to have several purposes. The fact it is commonest between males during the breeding season does not imply that it is simply a contest for mates which insures that the offspring are only fathered by the best fighters. There is widespread evidence of other rewards for the winners; on the one hand, rights to exclusive occupation of territory or, on the other hand, the establishment of rank in a

social hierarchy or "pecking order." Here we are concerned principally with territory and aggression; these other factors require separate consideration.

The way in which the right to territory and reproduction is established has been studied in many animals. A well documented example is the Red Grouse of the Scottish moors. These birds, which are vegetarians, live in heather on which they feed at about one grouse to each five acres. At the light of dawn on fine September mornings the cock-birds—old and young—gather in assemblies and joust for territory. The contest is mainly ritualistic; birds may face each other with their wings outstretched for periods of several hours and the losers usually give in without fighting. Soon the hens associate with the territorial cocks or fail to do so. Birds which do not gain territory become outcasts, are chased away by the owners of territory and become an easy prey for foxes and birds so that by the following spring 60 percent of all birds are dead. If cocks established in territories are shot, high ranking males among the outcasts move in to take their place.

A similar ritual by an African antelope has been described by Robert Ardrey. The males of the Uganda cob

meet on stamping grounds, each of which consists of a series of areas of close cropped grass about 50 feet in diameter—like a series of putting greens. The animals combat for possession of these territories; those near the center of the ground are more prized than those at the edge, and the ambitious young males at the fringe challenge, fight and wait to gain better locations. Only those males obtaining territory receive and mate with females. The female, says Ardrey, "wants affection, but she wants it at a good address."

Henry Howard likewise observed that among birds a male with a mate and no territory is an impossibility. In the animal kingdom at least it is not love that makes the world go around but territory. The parallel between human marriage and animal pairing is obvious. Equally apparent is the parallel between human desire for a place of one's own and animal instinct to stake out a private domain.

Love and Territory

This tangible human longing has a more persistent influence on our lives than is normally recognized. How many of us would be prepared to admit that a man has a closer affinity with the land he owns than the woman he lives with? Or to put it

Four territorial outrages! Whose newspaper is it, anyway? And why doesn't that guy keep his hands to himself? Just whose fishing spot is this? Finally, the character who came second should watch his feet!

another way, how many more men have died for their country in the course of history than have died for a woman? This truism which is valid on the national level is also relevant to our everyday domestic life; for the property held by two people transmits a fundamental strength to their enduring unity. Their union may have been formed and subsequently strengthened by sexual attraction, but it is the personal property of the parents that most satisfactorily insures the survival of their children.

The physical fact of ownership provides the man with extra reserves of energy for the protection of his family. Possession also means that both the man and woman remain locked in their own world and develop a mutual hostility for other members of the species. This enables them to focus their full attention on the needs of their children.

Is territory and its defense therefore more important than love to the human race? It would be reasonable to expect the power of love and loyalty to

remain, even when the family is no longer united by a common need for defense. But in order to discover the somber reality of continuing love and loyalty, we only have to remember an example. A family in which every relationship has been characterized by love, friendship and understanding is struck by death or divorce. Suddenly all these civilized sentiments disappear. In many instances there is no question of the members of the family being drawn closer together as a result of the tragedy; the insecurity it springs on them has a different effect and they become dominated by the need to grab as much territory as they can. This may take the shape of whole estates or houses, but is often confined to a vicious struggle for trivial items, such as furniture or cutlery. One of the strangest features of the territorial impulse is the physical form it may take.

The "place of our own" often comprises a small area of privacy more akin to a prison than a desirable territory: the automobile in city rush hours and the tenement slums of crowded cities are such examples. Yet, however "undesirable" the territory, man seems curiously attached to it. Newspapers continue to report instances of slum dwellers unwilling to relinquish their

territory and be "rehoused" in more salubrious conditions; of residents likewise resistant to new highways and airports when they threaten their houses. Man's defense of his territorial boundaries can be observed in an ever widening circle. We feel possessive about our house, our street, our town or suburb, our state or county, and our country. In time we will no doubt feel territorial about our planet!

You can explore the existence of the territorial imperative in human beings yourself:

Ask a married man what he would do if he was out with his wife and a strange man tried to become friendly with her.

Walk up to a secretary you do not know, open up one of her desk drawers, and take a piece of paper.

Ask a physician how he reacts when a patient makes a self-diagnosis and demands a specific medicine. (Watch what happens any time an "amateur" intrudes into an "expert's" field.)

Find a man sitting in his parked car and sit down on the front bumper bar of the car.

Walk up to a woman and drop a paper clip into her handbag.

Man...or beast?

Is man naturally aggressive, or does his environment trigger off violent emotions? Whatever the case, we must learn to channel and control our aggressive urges.

"If we put together, into the same container, two sticklebacks, lizards, robins, rats, monkeys or boys, who have not had any previous experience of each other, they will fight." So the noted animal behaviorist Konrad Lorenz sums up a disturbing facet of behavior that has concerned observers of animal and human societies for many centuries: aggression.

Destructive aggression, kind against kind, is not restricted to any single species but is a nearly universal blight on animals as well as primitive and modern men. According to the American professor of anthropology S. L. Washburn:

"The highest rate of killing so far recorded for any primate is that of the langur monkeys in South India; the adult males of this group kill infants of their own species. Rhesus monkeys kill rhesus monkeys at far higher rates than soldiers were killed in the [American] Civil War. All old, male baboons have scars and fractures of the kind received in male-male fights.

"In many preindustrial societies more than 20 percent of adult males were killed in intertribal conflict. The death rates in primitive raiding and war were far higher than in recent wars. The highest rates of murder, cannibalism, and infanticide were among Eskimo. In addition, many customs, such as head-hunting in Southeast Asia and nearby islands, involved killing as a prerequisite rite before a man could marry. In many tribes captives were tortured to death."

Modern man, despite the supposed progress of civilization, appears to be the most aggressive of creatures, destroying his own kind in a manner that can only be described as genocide. It has been calculated that in the 126 years between 1820 and 1945 at least 59 million human beings were killed in wars, murderous attacks and other deadly quarrels. This total is almost certainly an underestimate. A further catalogue of examples is not necessary to convince us that aggression poses a threat of a dimension we are only beginning to grasp in an age where total destruction is possible.

But recognizing a problem is just half the way to understanding and controlling it. We must first try to ascertain what it is in our make-up that causes us to be aggressive.

And, if we are to learn to manage our aggression, one question remains paramount, namely: is the drive to aggression in man instinctive, inherited as part of our animal ancestry, or is it only the result of frustration? If left unthreatened and in peace, would men behave peacefully—or is there a spontaneous drive to aggressive behavior which must somehow be accommodated?

Opinions differ widely. Many people, such as the animal behaviorists Konrad Lorenz, Irenaus Eibl-Eibesfeldt and Desmond Morris, the psychiatrist Anthony Storr and the writer Robert

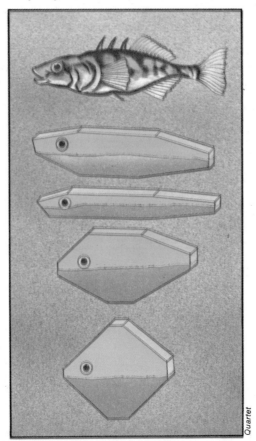

During the breeding season the male stickleback will drive away all territorial intruders. The fish, which develops a red throat, will attack wooden models painted red as shown above. It is the color, not the shape, which matters.

Ardrey, believe that men are innately aggressive and that they can only live in peace if their aggression can be understood. Others regard this hypothesis as an unworthy acceptance of innate depravity or original sin, holding that one cannot extrapolate from animals to men and that all human behavior is learned. This view springs mainly from a school of American psychologists, of whom Dr. J. Dollard was the prime mover, and is much favored by some sociologists for whom faith in the infinite malleability of the human organism is a political necessity.

Some psychologists think that dividing behavior into "instinctive" and "learned" categories is scientifically inadequate anyway. They believe that the term "learning" is too general and imprecise to be useful in establishing criteria for understanding behavior.

Man's basic instinctive patterns are so carefully covered by a complex structure of learned wishes, desires, beliefs, and other products of his brain that the most essential truths are hidden from consciousness. Thus it is indeed impossible to describe man's aggression in the same kind of terms which ethnologists use to describe animal actions.

Instinctive Reactions

Yet in man, as in animals, there is a physiological mechanism which, when stimulated, evokes subjective feelings of anger and causes physical changes which prepare the body for fighting. At the physiological level, two angry people resemble each other and, indeed, other animals; they make certain gestures and observable changes in their stance and expression, all of which are unconscious. This response can be called "instinctive"; but it is their training which determines how they will adapt to and control their aggression.

Perhaps the debate is, in any case, academic. Even if men are not spontaneously aggressive, their aggression is so easily activated and they are so rarely free of the frustration which releases aggression that we must treat them as potentially dangerous animals.

We can still learn much about the source of aggression by looking lower on the evolutionary scale. Wild animals are not, however, as destructive and rapacious as popularly believed. Carnivorous animals—such as lions, tigers, wolves, hawks and snakes—do, of course, kill and eat their prey; but hunting is not an act of hostility comparable with fighting since anger is not involved. Apart from the predator-prey relationship, animals belonging to different species normally ignore one another. On the other hand, animals of the same species often threaten each other and fight. This can be classed as violent behavior.

This kind of aggressive behavior is as necessary for survival as hunting and killing of prey; it is undoubtedly connected with natural selection and, far from being destructive, has biological advantages. The stronger members of a species fight to gain territory and mates, basic necessities for survival, weeding out the weaker members and thus ensuring the continuance of the species. They, and by extension we, are equipped with a natural, protective, aggression.

Biological Causes

The African antelope's ritualized combat for choice territory may seem far removed from human behavior, unless we consider our own jealous disputes over neighbors' boundaries, to say nothing of oil lands or outlets to the sea. Man is a territorial animal himself, and the entire structure of his personality and his society contrives to defend what is his against all intruders. And no one needs much convincing that the human mating game is as perilous and competitive as anything ever observed in the animal kingdom.

There is further evidence that a source of aggression is biological: a few kinds of violence are unquestionably the result of diagnosable disease or are associated with recognizable physiological abnormalities of the brain. An extreme example is the disease *encephalitis lethargica*, which affected many children during the year 1920. Within a few months of recovery, particularly in children aged between three and ten years, there were profound alterations in be-

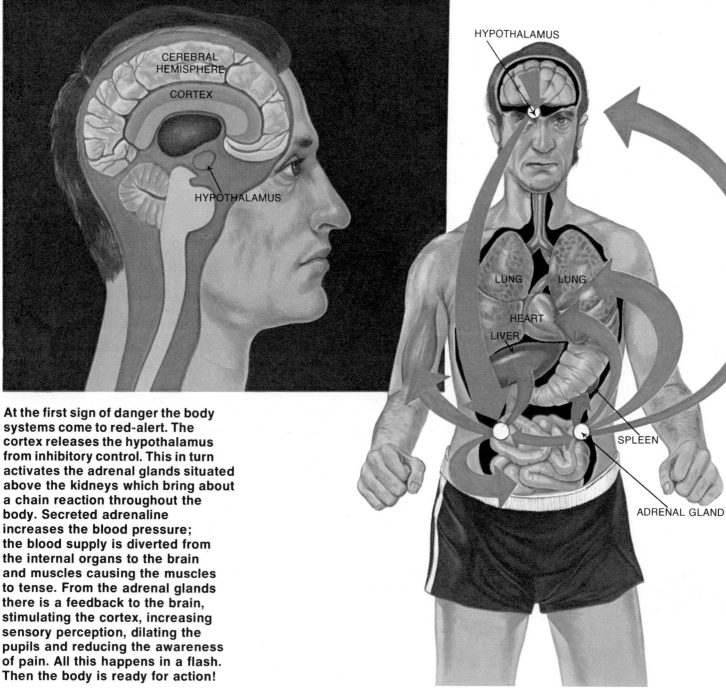

At the first sign of danger the body systems come to red-alert. The cortex releases the hypothalamus from inhibitory control. This in turn activates the adrenal glands situated above the kidneys which bring about a chain reaction throughout the body. Secreted adrenaline increases the blood pressure; the blood supply is diverted from the internal organs to the brain and muscles causing the muscles to tense. From the adrenal glands there is a feedback to the brain, stimulating the cortex, increasing sensory perception, dilating the pupils and reducing the awareness of pain. All this happens in a flash. Then the body is ready for action!

Ron Hayward

havior. The children, who had previously behaved normally, would lie, steal, destroy and set fire to property, and commit sexual offenses, without thought of punishment. Often they made murderous attacks on others and sometimes mutilated themselves, and it became necessary to set up special institutions throughout the world to care for and protect them.

A Surgical Solution

Aggressive behavior in cats and dogs can be greatly increased by surgical interference with parts of the brain which thus normally appear to exercise an inhibiting influence. Similarly, impulsiveness, irritability and intolerance of frustration are found in human patients with certain brain lesions, and they are especially marked in a state known as temporal lobe epilepsy. In this condition, which sometimes results from a difficult birth, children show extreme bad temper which later may change to anxiety, depression, hallucinations, feelings of persecution, or sexual perversion. On the other hand, an operation known as prefrontal leucotomy, in which certain brain connections are severed, not only makes patients less anxious, but, as far as self-directed violence —mutilation or suicide—is concerned, less aggressive.

Aggressive Drive in Children

The facts make it clear that hostile behavior is elicited and inhibited by different regions of the brain, and that it can be greatly influenced by brain damage. But even without signs of physical damage to the brain, some people—so-called "aggressive psychopaths"—appear unable to control their hostile impulses. Between a quarter and half of them show abnormal electrical rhythms of the brain, as recorded by the electroencephalogram. An interesting example was Neville Heath, hanged in England in 1946 for two brutal murders, who had a history of psychopathic abnormality since childhood.

Likewise, some aggressive behavior may have a genetic component. Studies in hospitals for criminal insanity have shown that about two percent of the patients have abnormalities of the sex chromosomes. Though the extent of such genetic abnormality is not yet fully established, it seems likely that tendencies to violent behavior may be inherited.

This evolutionary and physical evidence suggests that aggression is so deep-seated in the animal nature that external circumstances do nothing

more than evoke a tendency that is always darkly present below the surface of even the most civilized beings.

Certainly, children are aggressive from birth; babies are notoriously angry—or at least they seem so— screaming, kicking, raging, before any learning or conditioning can take place. They are equipped from the beginning for survival. As soon as the child can move around and explore, it begins to develop its independence by extending its confrontation to the external world. Aggressive drives thus appear to be a natural part of the

Study in aggression and submission. Above, a man who looks ready for a fight or at least angry words adopts a bold stance. He wants it known he will take no nonsense and is prepared to stand his ground no matter what happens. But at right a man adopts a stooping, submissive pose, clenching his hands together in front of him to show he will not use them as weapons. Research has revealed that trouble starts when a person can find no way of expressing aggression. Submission then turns into aggression.

endeavor to master the environment and play an important role in personality development.

Growing up and achieving independence requires a degree of self-assertion and aggression. A child at first depends on its mother as the source of infinite love and support. Later he comes to realize that his mother can be a source of frustration as well as love, and his growing aggression is periodically directed against her. This aggression is part of the mechanism by which separation from the mother is achieved. But after the aggression is spent, love returns; paradoxically, it is the assurance of that love which allows the drive to independence.

Some psychologists hold that aggression would disappear if frustrations were removed, and therefore believe that children should never be restrained or reprimanded but given the maximum liberty. This method of rearing children often results in their becoming more aggressive and disturbed than those subjected to discipline. Stability for the child requires

Kim Sayer

that his aggression shall have opposition; the urge towards independence needs a firm—though not frightening —authority against which to rebel.

The culture of children also shows a content of aggression. Games are usually struggles in which the child can identify itself with one side or the other, and indeed the development of moral attitudes reflects the conflict of "good" and "evil" as exemplified by the good fairy and the demon king in old-fashioned pantomime, or the heroes and villains in cowboy films. Stories and comics are full of aggressive fantasies, often containing violence which children enjoy but parents find disturbing. However, there is no satisfactory evidence that a diet of violence makes children more aggressive or, indeed, that violence in society is the result of horror comics or television, any more than elderly maiden ladies are driven to crime by reading detective stories.

Releasing Aggression

They may, however, elicit a hostile response from an already overly aggressive person and for that reason could be dangerous; yet some psychologists believe that violence in films, for example, serves as a safety valve for pent-up aggression and that viewers express their own hostility vicariously by watching the "bad guy" get beaten.

Studies have shown that it is when a person cannot find an outlet for his aggressive tendencies that they cause trouble. The more dominated and less assertive a child—or indeed a nation —the angrier and more destructive it becomes. In addition to the universal need for development through aggression, modern society builds up a hundred frustrations in us every day. A man working off his aggression by digging in the garden or playing baseball on a Saturday is instinctively doing the right thing. He gives his rage time to subside while at the same time expending some of the physical energy frustration has built up in his combat-alerted body.

The inability to become adjusted to one's aggressive impulses can be manifested in several ways. They may be repressed and turned inwards resulting in depression, a state which many otherwise normal people experience from time to time, but which at the extreme may lead to suicide. Or a person may withdraw completely from human contact and refuse to enter into any emotional relationship because it is seen as a threat, exhibiting the so-called schizoid personality.

At the other extreme, he may attribute his own hostility to others, believing himself to be persecuted and reacting to this by hatred and cruelty; this condition is described as paranoid schizophrenia.

Schizoid personalities, in withdrawing both their love and their aggression from others, conceal a contempt for them behind their indifference. They often feel superior to the remainder of the human race and they are particularly sensitive to any criticism of that superiority. They often become successful political leaders or great artists. Perhaps, like the late General De Gaulle, they believe themselves to be the embodiment of their national glory, or like Stalin suffer illusions of grandeur; perhaps, like Beethoven, they may contribute their genius to the arts. To compensate for the failure of love by acts of creation is clearly a greater—and safer—contribution to the human estate than to aspire to absolute political power.

The most dangerous person to society is, however, the paranoid schizophrenic, and an examination of his personality throws considerable light on the nature of human cruelty. Instead of withdrawal, the paranoid schizophrenic accommodates his own hostility by believing himself to be persecuted by others, either by individuals or by other identifiable groups. There is thus a desire to be revenged; and although this hostility is usually not expressed in action, it can sometimes lead to murder.

Mastering Life

Feelings of this kind are not confined to the obviously insane. The tendency to find a scapegoat as an excuse for one's failure and on which to vent one's aggression is universal—not one of us is totally free from it.

Yet while aggression has been a constant and widespread source of friction and destruction, it is at the same time a natural and necessary force to maintain life. According to Clara Thomson, an American analyst, "Aggression is not necessarily destructive at all. It springs from an innate tendency to grow and master life, which seems to be characteristic of all living matter."

It is only when these natural tendencies go uncontrolled and unchanneled, whether for physical or psychological reasons, that they spill over into the hostilities we have learned to fear from each other, that inhibit rather than enhance life and mark the difference between stimulating competition and savage attack.

Topix

Zoological Society of London

How necessary is aggression?

The passion for aggression seems to be necessary for the survival of both man and animals as species. But human hostility can be transformed into acts of universal benefit.

The terrifying specter of an atomic explosion and the glory of the civilization of Ancient Greece may seem to have mercifully little to do with each other. One speaks of the most inhuman hostility, the other of such fruitful cooperation that it seems inconceivable that they might be linked. Yet, paradoxically, each has a common source in human aggression and competition.

Many behaviorists in fact believe that aggression is at the very root of our survival as a species, our maturation as individuals, and the establishment of productive societies.

Our nearest animal relatives, the apes and monkeys, are organized in social groups. For example, baboon troops having up to 200 members show well-established hierarchies, and although the rank order is brought about by aggressive interactions, it results in a peaceful community, for each animal knows its place and if fighting does break out the dominant males usually suppress it. Moreover the social structure helps orderly mobilization of the whole group if it is attacked from the outside by other animals such as leopards, and it provides a framework within which young animals learn from the more experienced animals.

Growth of Social Order

The success of human evolution seems to have depended on the coherence of social groups. Most early societies were based on rank orders, each man, from chief, king or emperor, dominating and directing his aggression towards his immediate inferior, down to the lowliest.

While it may be true that modern democratic states embody the ideal of equality of all subjects before the law, it is obvious that they retain many hierarchical features. Moreover, as Dr. Anthony Storr has pointed out, they have the problem of how to reorientate the aggression of their members. This is achieved, not always with complete success, by the creation of an internal opposition and competition. It is then possible for men of like political persuasion to cooperate in striving against those of different opinion, or for others to surpass their rivals in achieving distinction—or money, and so group energy focuses on a common goal for all. The greatest achievements of civilization are born either of competition or the desire to excel or both—from Michelangelo's *David* to the alto-mobile. Without this challenge, men and societies stagnate. In societies that do not allow internal differences, like Fascist states, aggression is focused outwards, fostering cooperation within the group, but causing havoc without. Indeed, the one seems to depend on the other; the greater the external pressure on a social group for whatever reason, then the greater is the internal cohesion.

The results are devastating enough when an individual fails to control his aggressive impulses; when the normal mechanics for social aggression go awry, the consequences can be disastrous and end in the annihilation of whole nations.

Organized violence, in which members of a group cooperate with each other but compete aggressively with outsiders, is widespread in man and has its parallel in other animals. Chimpanzees cooperate within a troop but are aggressive towards other troops; human examples range from the family feud which separated Romeo and Juliet to modern gang warfare. Frequently the formation of a group increases the level of aggression, restrained individual behavior giving way to mob psychology or "lynch law." Aggressive behavior is often displayed by teenage youths who fight in bands or form squads to bait homosexuals, Jews, or other subjects with supposedly alien values.

Persecution and War

Such behavior is, unfortunately, not confined to immature adolescents. The identification and torture of scapegoats has been and still is a feature of human establishments, whether political or religious. Frequently, justification of the procedures is claimed in the interests of society. The medieval Ecclesiastical Courts and the Holy Inquisition really believed that they were saving the souls of heretics as well as protecting other Christians from contamination by evil; in fact, they broke their bodies with thumbscrews, racks and vices before burning them alive—unless the subjects confessed. Then they were granted the mercy of strangulation before consignment to the flames.

The Nazis were able to persuade masses of ordinary German people to project their deep paranoid fears on the Jews and to accept as true the most unlikely fantasies about them. Jews were accused not only of seeking world power by financial domina-

tion but of being murderers and poisoners and a threat to the purity of the "Aryan race." In consequence they were deprived of civil rights and herded in concentration camps; the final solution—their extermination in gas chambers—was so horrible that many closed their minds to the possibility; but it happened, clearly demonstrating the existence of schizoid tendencies deep in ordinary people.

There is undoubtedly no more frightening manifestation of organized aggression than war. The problems of overpopulation, starvation and destruction of the environment creep on us gradually and their urgency escapes many, but the shadow of the hydrogen bomb is terrible and imminent. Has war always been part of the human scene? Is it a rational part of human activity with defined methods and achievable ends, or is it the ultimate irrational extension of our aggressive drives? Can it be eradicated or at least contained?

The answers to these questions are neither clear nor universally agreed. Its long history, its wide distribution and the enthusiasm with which some past conflicts have been enjoined, suggest that men may have an innate propensity towards war. Yet it may also be argued that if this were so,

A baboon tribe has a rigid "pecking order"; and sociologists see the same hierarchy among humans—Hell's Angels and politicians alike, despite aggressive competition within the group, maintain strict social discipline.

no nation would remain at peace for more than a generation. Nor would it be necessary for political rulers to stimulate martial ardor by playing upon vanity and fear of contempt, or exhorting group loyalty, or maintaining conscription. Perhaps a few men are warlike and most are not. History, in retrospect, certainly could endow these with undue bellicosity. In the seventeenth to nineteenth centuries, for example, though European nations waged dozens of wars to furnish the history books, the soldiers who actually fought in them made up less than one percent of the total population of the countries involved.

There is insufficient evidence to decide when war originated in human evolution. Some authors have made much of evidence that fossil skulls of the early forerunners of man, apes of the genus *Australopithecus*, often show signs of violence which could have been inflicted by stone hand axes. On the other hand, some believe

Leimbach

pears to be in other animals a mechanism for ritualization of combat and submission of the vanquished that prevents actual destruction.

Occasionally fights between animals end in the mutilation or death of one of the protagonists; for example, male Indian elephants can mortally wound one another, and mutual slaughter of hippopotamuses has been described under conditions of great overcrowding along African rivers. But such destructive aggression is very rare. Throughout the animal kingdom fighting is normally intensely ritualized and consists more of threatening display than overt violence—exercises in bluff in which the loser gives way by making a gesture of submission or trials of strength conducted by stereotyped routines using specially evolved weapons. The clash of antlers as two roaring stags push against one another is a splendid show, more akin to a stage fight than a gladiatorial contest; it satisfies aggressive impulses and yet avoids unnecessary loss of life.

Controlling Human Destruction

Though this is not the general intent or result in human warfare, it would be wrong to assume that whereas animals ritualize their quarrels and live, men only fight ruthlessly and die. Diplomacy and warfare are intensely ritualistic. The posturing of politicians, the exchanging of notes, the conference tables, the walk-outs—all outstrip the antics of the animal kingdom. And the ritual is seen in the historical trappings of war—the beat of martial music and the threat posed by military uniforms, in which epaulettes are used to broaden the shoulders (just as dogs or apes enlarge the body profile by erecting the hair), and plumes or spikes are worn on the head to increase the height.

Warfare has, throughout its history, been far from total. Curiously, those societies that have not questioned the value of war as an institution have often been the most successful in restricting and regulating it. In Europe in the seventeenth century, for example, the savage freebootery of the late Middle Ages was replaced by a growth of professional armies. Europe became a military civilization. Professional soliders had every reason to develop rules of conduct both for their own survival, and as a matter of public relations. Civilians, as far as possible, were not to be involved; rape and pillage could no longer be the rewards of victorious troops. Thus the convention arose that a commander

that the early hominoids, who lived at low densities, were nonviolent, noble savages. We can only conclude that it is possible that the ancestors of man engaged in violent competition, but that there is no unquestionable proof that they did so.

Nor can the issue be settled on the anthropological evidence of existing tribes. Warfare is indeed widespread among the few primitive peoples remaining in the twentieth century. For example, the Willigiman-Wallala of the Baliem valley in western New Guinea, according to a Harvard University expedition which studied them, led lives which were "an unending round of death and revenge." Another tribe, the Kurelu, maintained almost constant war with a related tribe called the Wattaia. The two tribes lived so close to each other that they could shout insults, and they frequently sent out raiding parties to stalk and kill any individual—young or old and of either sex—of the other tribe. But there are also some races among whom aggressive behavior and war are rare.

Usually these are backward groups, living under the influence of overtly aggressive neighbors, which seem to have adapted themselves for survival by submission. Not surprisingly, similar characteristics are also shown by

very isolated people. Such are the members of a small group in the Philippines, the Tasaday, who appear to have been innocent of the outside world for at least 600 years, until their cave was discovered by anthropologists. They lack all belligerence, have no weapons, and do not even kill mammals for food or take the eggs from birds; living otherwise like Stone Age people, they eat mainly fruit.

Can War be Avoided?

If the nature of the connection between organized warfare by nations and the aggressive drive of individuals remains in doubt, there are several reasons for thinking they may be linked. Firstly, while it is possible to ascribe to wars political and economic causes, such causes frequently exist without open conflict. Secondly, wars which in the passion of their time seemed necessary or at least inevitable may in retrospect appear to have been irrationally sparked off or avoidable. In any case, whether or not men are driven to war by an innate violence, it is clear that once engaged in it their aroused aggression can lead them to destroy their fellows with great ruthlessness.

Fortunately, boding well for the survival of the human species, there ap-

who did not surrender his city when it had become indefensible could be court-martialled and executed on capture, but a garrison which gracefully surrendered could be accorded the "Honors of War" and allowed to march out with colors flying.

The Breakdown of Ritualization

In spite of the growth of international organizations, warfare seems to have become bloodier with the approach of universal democracy during the last two centuries. The growth of nationalism, mass conscription and the demands for total victory and unconditional surrender suggest that the only object of a modern nation at war is to win at any cost. Wars are no longer the extension of diplomacy by other means, professionally fought according to rules and with limited objectives. Now public opinion needs to be gratified or be aroused; wars have become crusades, laced with emotional appeals to national pride and moral indignation.

In the seventeenth century a Turkish leader, having defeated the Russians led by Peter the Great, rejected any idea that their army should be destroyed and the Czar seized, saying, "Who then would govern his people and with whom should we deal?" Yet in the twentieth century it was supposedly enlightened public opinion in Britain and America which demanded the prosecution of the Second World War until the unconditional surrender of the enemy. It could be that our protective ritualization is ebbing away the more we evolve away from our animal roots.

If men are not innately aggressive, but—as some historians believe—resort to war for definable reasons, then our aim must be to eliminate the economic and political causes of war. But if, on the other hand, warfare fulfills some innate drive to aggression, it would be unwise not to recognize this and to look for means of accommodating it. Within nations, some progress towards ritualizing men's individual aggression has been made. The problem remains to devise successful rituals, short of overt violence, like the Space Race or the

Left: Organized competition like the Olympic Games could help to channel aggression and prevent wars. Right: Uniforms are worn in all cultures. In combat, man, like most animals, instinctively emphasizes the fearsomeness of his body; plumes and padding enhance the warrior's size and height.

47

Angus McBride

Olympic Games to resolve aggressive competition between nations.

Dr. Anthony Storr has suggested that the United Nations'or some other international organization set aside funds to start a series of annual contests. The countries might vie for the best-built mental hospital, the safest car, the best-designed house—a far more productive and safer form of competition.

The evidence we have examined suggests that although human violence can be a frightening phenomenon, aggressive competition has a large part to play in human affairs and that its effects are by no means all disadvantageous. Is it possible to have an entirely noncompetitive society? Certainly, many have believed so, and attempts have been made to create it. Whether men have an innate urge to aggression which must be accommodated, or whether their aggression arises from frustration which could be relieved if only the environment were altered, is a continuing debate. But, on the face of it, it looks as if the same impulse which can lead to destruction may also be the driving force towards human achievement and the future development of society.

Competition and Achievement

The history of man is the history of his social institutions. To create the universal society, it is often suggested that barriers between ethnic, religious, trade and other groups ought to be broken down to make the roads to salvation, the choice of profession, and group membership freely available to all. Yet men and women create their own identities in such forms of association and they make rules to restrict the entry of others. When the group becomes too large, or membership too easy to obtain, the original members either form another group with a new and restricted identity, or they engage in passionate dispute among themselves, as the histories of the Christian churches and the communist ideologies show.

It seems, therefore, that the maintenance of both social structure and human identity depends upon controversy and competition. If enemies do not exist it may be necessary to create them; it follows that they ought not to be destroyed. In the words of Anthony Storr, "Man can only be safe from strife when in the womb or in the grave: both fine and private places which we may long for or regret. But in the one the dynamic life has hardly yet begun, whilst in the other it has disappeared forever."

The fiercer sex

Sugar and spice? Actually, little girls are quite likely to be "mean and hostile," and, with today's greater freedom, are growing up to be increasingly aggressive. This aggression is reflected in more serious crimes among teenage girls, more serious driving offenses among adult women.

It is clear from their earliest months that boys and girls may differ quite markedly in their aggressive behavior, and in a way that cannot be glibly assigned to role conditioning. Even in the first year there are differences in physical aggressiveness. The baby boy is far more adventurous in exploring heights, seeking the unknown and delving into the many hazards that line the modern house.

Boys also tend to look tougher and more aggressive than their sisters. "Oh, he's a real boy, you couldn't mistake him for a girl," inevitably means that, at an age when it is often difficult to tell which sex is which, a tough little face and squared shoulders are automatic signs of aggressive masculinity.

From quite an early age boys gang up together and play violent games—cops and robbers, cowboys and Indians. Playing with toy soldiers, space suits and guns comes much more naturally to boys than to girls. Although the solitary boy may be quite happy with his sister's doll's house and tea parties, he soon discards them when playing with other boys.

An experiment showed how groups of boys and girls reacted towards a large inflatable doll. As might be expected, the boys attacked and pummeled the doll far more than the girls. On average the boys struck the doll 28 times compared with the girls' 4.5 blows.

The physical changes around puberty strikingly herald the boy's physically more aggressive role. The feminine form becomes rounded and more gentle. The hips widen, anticipating her childbearing function. The boy's form is more muscular, making him generally stronger physically—with his narrower hips and more streamlined body he is equipped for hunting and fighting.

Girls—"Mean and Hostile"?

Aggressiveness, however, is not only physical in nature. Although boys are directly and actively aggressive—if John wants Jim's bike, he will push him off it until one or other of them submits and hands over—girls may be "mean and hostile" in some circumstances.

This was effectively demonstrated in a further experiment. Pairs of young boys and girls were set to play together with various toys. All be-

From child to adult. A comparison of the bodily development of a boy and a girl up to maturity, illustrating the overt physical changes. It can be seen how the male differs from the female at each distinct stage in development. The male normally takes on a more strikingly aggressive appearance.

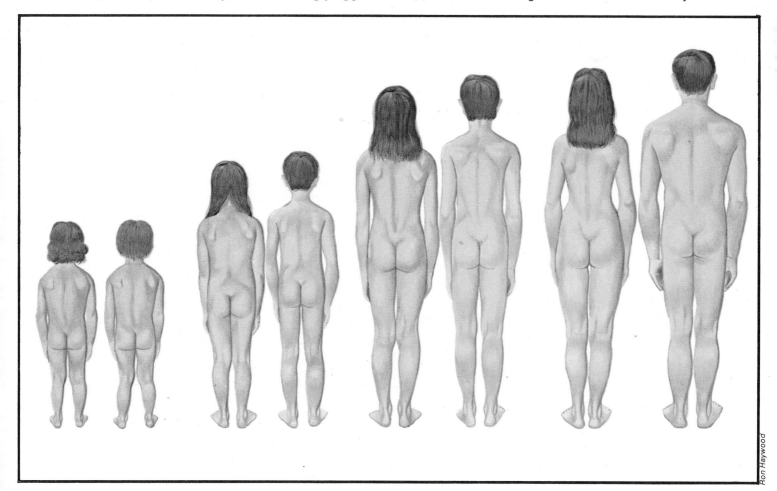

Ron Haywood

haved amicably without any striking displays of aggression until a newcomer was introduced. It was expected that the boys might be more outwardly aggressive—though the fact that the children knew adults were around may have affected this—but there were no significant differences between the sexes.

However, the girls were initially more unkind and unfriendly towards the newcomer, especially when the newcomer was a boy. Several of them did not make a single approach, many showed some disdain and one girl even tried to terrorize him by stalking him around the room, rolling her eyes.

Older 13- and 14-year-old boys and girls confirmed these differences in another experiment. Pairs of friends had to solve a task with an outsider. Only 4 out of 15 female pairs accepted a newcomer's ideas in their final solution compared with 10 out of 14 male pairs.

The Mating Game

Academically girls can be just as competitive and aggressive as boys—indeed those who go from school to college often do better than their male counterparts. But only a few carry this competitive aggressiveness through after leaving college. It is striking how often apparently brilliant girls, who seemed fired with the desire to succeed, marry on finishing their studies and then abandon further study or competitive achievement.

It is tempting to suggest that, with some at least, their determination and aggression in succeeding academically are unconsciously a form of competitiveness among other females in order to secure a better mate. Having succeeded, this form of aggressive behavior fades away, to be replaced by other priorities.

The psychologist's arguments over whether aggression is innate or learned is irrelevant in this context. Like a facility for language, aggression is an instinct that is then formed in specific ways by the learning process. What remains constant in virtually all human societies is the harmonious imbalance between the

Behavioral studies have demonstrated that male and female children placed in the same situation react in totally different ways. A girl (top) will usually just sit in a playpen, not attempting to explore. But a boy (bottom) will probably move around more and at some point will try to stand up or climb out.

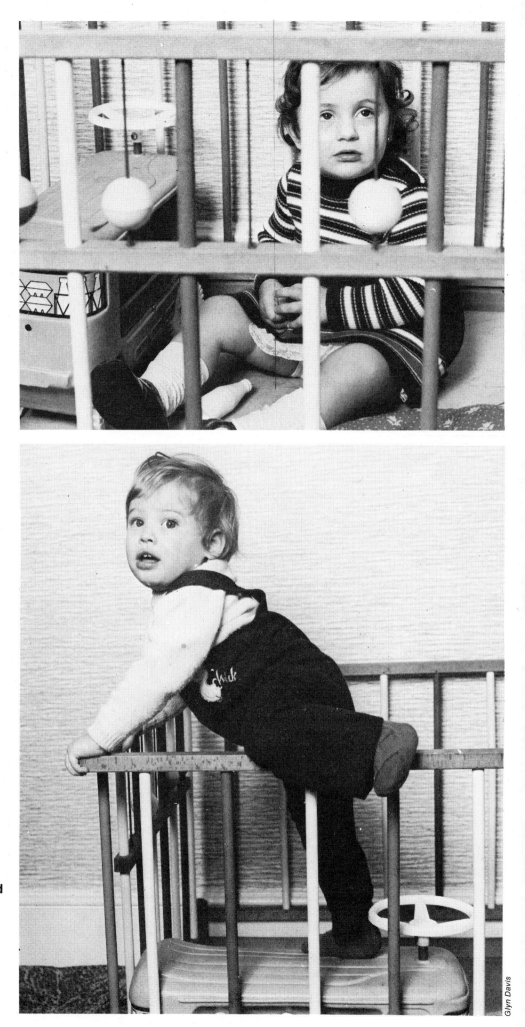

Glyn Davis

aggressiveness of men and women.

Psychologists and psychiatrists in the main agree that this imbalance is the essential cornerstone to the only satisfactory human unit yet devised —the family. We shall see what happens when the aggressive male/submissive female relationship is reversed. Most of us instinctively feel that there is something "wrong" when we see the mild, hen-pecked man struggling along under an armful of groceries, being abused for his stupidity or slowness by a formidable wife.

> The full grown man is clearly more aggressive than a woman, in that he is both more violent and more ambitious. When a society goes to war, it recruits its strong men as soldiers; combatant female soldiers are normally only found among guerillas, who belong to a threatened and struggling minority and are under great pressure to utilize all their resources.

While the concept of the caveman with his club is equally funny, it does not offend our sense of what is right.

There are, of course, occasional successful families in which the wife/mother is totally dominant in the role normally fulfilled by the man. She may be widowed or divorced or the breadwinner while her husband stays at home. If everything else is right, the child will normally be able to adapt to this reversal of the general truth he finds in the outside world.

It is on this difference in aggressiveness that the "battle of the sexes" is based. Aggressiveness is the characteristic in which a man differs most obviously from a woman, and as such is frequently confused with the concept of superiority. It is, therefore, an area of intense concern for the Women's Liberation Movement, which sometimes believes that true equality should mean exact equality.

At its most basic level this simply does not make common sense. With his superior muscle a man is obviously a better candidate for the building site than a woman, while those who have been in hospital will say they prefer being nursed by a woman rather than a man. There are areas of sex discrimination, but it is unhelpful to ignore inherent physical and psychological differences.

As an evolutionary force, this male aggressiveness serves in the competition and selection of the best (fittest, cleverest and most attractive)

females. It was constantly reinforced by man's need to go out and hunt or search for food, making him gregarious and aggressive. Woman stayed at home and guarded the young—developing strong protective feelings—and becoming really aggressive only when her children and home were threatened.

In more recent times this difference has meant that man has made up the rules of the game, so that for a woman to succeed in direct competition—as for example a top government official or president of a company—she must develop what are normally considered male characteristics. Again we (both men and women) tend to see this as unnatural and shudder at the concept of a woman boss.

This is true even in intensely feminine professions. A nurse is a symbol of femininity, the protecting, gentle healer on the one hand and the desirable girl friend on the other. Yet the matron, who has achieved the ultimate nursing position, is characterized as a tough dragon.

It is fashionable to believe that women are incapable of the highest creativity: there has never been a female Mozart or Rubens, runs the argument. Yet it is in those areas where aggressiveness is not at such a premium that woman emerges most clearly as man's equal—in medicine, scientific research and literature. It can be suggested that only time and overall female emancipation are needed for women to produce geniuses in creative fields. After all, it has taken millions of emancipated men over many centuries to throw up what geniuses there have been so far.

> The administration of male hormones to young animals makes them more aggressive, and castration makes them docile. Farmers do not keep herds of bulls together, and when they want to train them for work they castrate them. In many animal species—including humans—the male looks more aggressive and has stronger muscles and a fiercer face.

This is a less obvious function of aggressiveness, but as Dr. Anthony Storr pointed out in his book, *Human Aggression*, we use aggressive terms to describe intellectual and artistic achievements—"mastering" subjects, "fighting" a problem, "overcoming" its difficulties with our "sharpened" wits. One school of thought—based

on Freud—believes that aggressiveness is always in response to frustration, but this is hard to sustain when one considers the positive drive in man to conquer fresh intellectual and artistic frontiers.

> On the whole women tend to admire men who are aggressive, who compete successfully in work and play with contemporaries who are also their rivals. The stereotyped picture of the small-town buck, qualifying to join the local firm of lawyers, captaining the sports team, and sweeping the pretty daughter of the town's wealthiest businessman off her feet, has much truth to it.
>
> Men are normally attracted by the kind of aggression that makes a woman stand out from her friends. One can think of the girl who sparkles at parties, dresses well and perhaps drives a fast sports car.

More primitive primates live in simple societies, and the most aggressive male will be the sexually superior animal and leader in other ways. Man lives in many hierarchies—at home, at work, with his friends—and it is not inconsistent for a man to be at the same time both an assertive, successful businessman and a meek husband. Even where the husband is obviously the dominant partner, there will be times when the roles are reversed—in a shop perhaps, or when his wife's friends come in for coffee.

Each human needs the emotional security of knowing that he or she is valued correctly and has a secure role in each of the hierarchies they inhabit. It is when the structure breaks that the uncertainty—and often with it violence—occurs.

Where a girl's experience is the same as a boy's, she will develop many aggressive characteristics associated with boys. More teenage girls are being convicted of crimes of considerable severity: a leading psychiatrist explained it in terms of the comparative freedom girls are now allowed. Instead of having to be in by a certain time, they are more likely to roam the streets as late as their brothers.

This creates the opportunity (and provides the example) for getting involved with gangs that carry out house-breaking or even mugging. Some girls are going beyond fringe involvement with boys and forming their own teams to initiate crimes. Traditionally, women have sat at home in the passive role of receivers of stolen goods.

Similarly, the rate of increase in convictions of adult women for serious (and therefore usually aggressive) driving offenses is very rapid, though still remaining a tiny part of the total number of motoring crimes.

These changes in behavior and aspiration are highly relevant to sexual relationships. In many animal species, the more aggressive male fights—usually in accepted ritual—other males for sexual supremacy. Young boys, scarcely conscious of their sexual drives, may be wrestling light-heartedly when girls come to watch. Instinctively, the fight will assume an aggressive, competitive edge.

Faint Heart and Fair Lady

Conventionally, the man has gone out and "won his woman": "None but the brave deserves the fair." This simple concept is complicated by the modern blurring of clearly defined sexual roles. The career woman will give out different "signals" at her job than she will in her guise as a potential mother. This confusion of roles has developed relatively quickly, leaving considerable bewilderment in

The structures built by boys and girls differ considerably in concept and shape. For example, a male child given a set of blocks to play with will commonly arrange them in a characteristically masculine manner. The structural shapes he assembles (top)

tend to be more phallic, bold, and outgoing. But girls put the blocks together (bottom) into more enclosed shapes, much as if they were making a cozy home. And boys tire of their creations quickly, breaking them up. Girls want them to last longer.

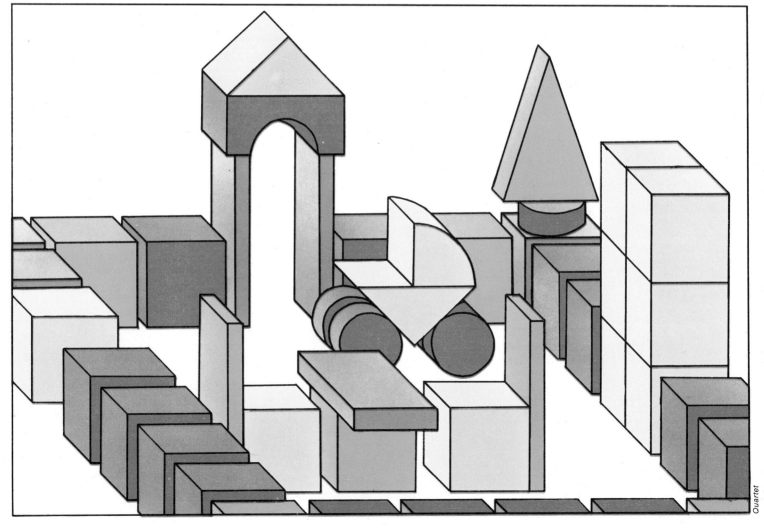

Quartet

Marshall Cavendish

quite a few of her many relationships.

The man's active role is symbolized by the sexual act. He penetrates the woman and his sperm swims to her passive egg. Fear of women causes impotence or sexual inhibitions. A man totally dominated by his mother may often seek a dominant wife in an attempt to recreate the one secure relationship he has known. The insecure man, frightened to commit himself, will usually appear timid.

Jealous Love

The insecure woman is more likely to hide her uncertainty by being aggressive. She resents the male and is unconsciously competing with him. She will try to rouse his manliness through her own aggression, but will almost certainly inhibit him yet further, reinforcing his fears. She is seeking domination, and so is he.

Children can usually play together amicably without showing too much aggression if they know one another. At left a girl happily paints as her playmate looks on. Boys (right) also get along well. But things change when a newcomer appears.

In the unbalanced sexual relationship the timid man is suppressing his aggressiveness, while the dominant woman is expressing hers. The man will find an outlet in bursts of often irrational irritability and moods of depression when his aggression turns in on himself.

When there is tremendous dependence allied to passionate feeling—as, in another context, in the small underground political group or small radical religious society—there is always the possibility of vicious dissent over the slightest thing.

Similarly between sexual partners, when the love turns to hate, there is an explosive accumulation of feelings that makes *crimes passionels* among the most common forms of murder.

The more dependent the person is on the love, the more threatened and therefore hostile he is if the relationship breaks up. The jealous lover who takes a gun and shoots his unfaithful girl friend is the man who was too dependent.

Utopians, who visualize the perfect world as devoid of aggressiveness, probably have not considered the role it plays in normal circumstances. If aggressiveness were not necessary for human survival, evolution would have eliminated it. It is the supreme irony that such an essential human force should also—with the aid of nuclear weapons—pose the greatest threat to mankind.

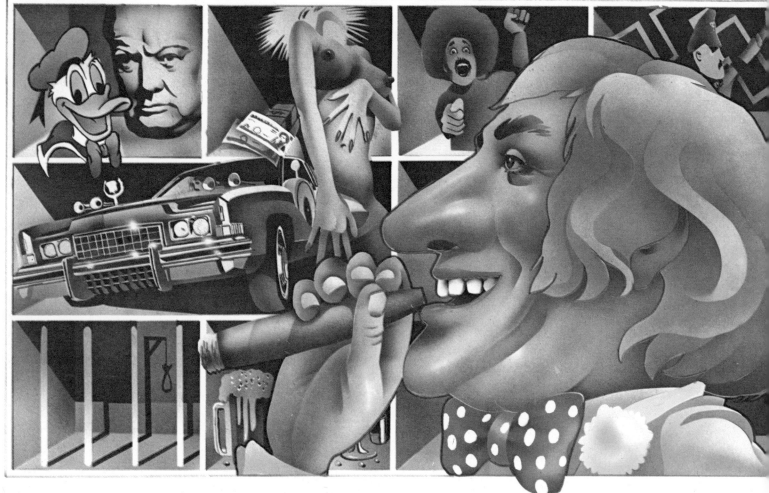

Extrovert or Introvert?

This is a picture of some well-known characters and personalities. All of them are either extroverts or introverts. So what kind of personality are you?

What kind of personality do you have? This is an enormously complex question. It involves not only the kind of person the rest of the world thinks you to be, but also the kind of person you really are. An answer to the problem of personality must further take into account the fact that everyone on earth is in some way unique. There is no one else exactly like him. Even physically identical twins do not have identical personalities.

The late Gordon Allport, one of America's leading experts on personality and individuality, once searched a dictionary for words used to characterize personalities. He produced a list of more than a thousand, each of which could be used to describe some aspect of a person's uniqueness.

The problem of self-knowledge has occupied mankind for more than 2,500 years. Hippocrates, the "father of medicine" who lived some 400 years before Christ, is usually credited with first formulating the Greek theory that everyone could be placed pre-

cisely into one of four types—the sanguine (cheerful), melancholic (sad), choleric (angry) and phlegmatic (calm).

However, the fact that everyone had to fit neatly into one of four personality pigeonholes was a fundamental weakness of the Greek theory. It left no room for shades of personality. Yet this is contrary to our experience. Most people we meet have complex personalities. They seem to combine features from two, or even three, of the basic Greek types.

Extroverts and Introverts

A more sophisticated and flexible modern approach to the problem—and probably the best—has used "types" popularized by the Swiss psychiatrist Carl Gustav Jung. This means that everyone—including you—can find his niche somewhere on a scale running from extreme extroversion (outgoing personality) to extreme introversion (withdrawn personality).

The extrovert is a person who

values both the material and immaterial things of the world (possessions, riches, power, prestige). He is sociable, likes parties, has many friends, needs to have people to talk to, does not like reading or studying by himself. He craves excitement, takes chances, often sticks his neck out, acts on the spur of the moment and is generally an impulsive person. He moves his home more frequently, changes jobs more frequently, is low on "brand loyalty." He is fond of practical jokes, always has a ready answer and generally likes new things, new people, new impressions. He is carefree, optimistic and likes to "laugh and be merry." He prefers to keep moving and doing things, tends to be aggressive and loses his temper quickly. Altogether, his feelings are not kept under tight control, and he is not always a reliable person. He may often be subject to criminal or psychopathic behavior.

The typical introvert, on the other hand, is a quiet, retiring sort of per-

Philip Castle

son, introspective, fond of books rather than people. He is reserved and distant except with intimate friends. He tends to plan ahead, "looks before he leaps," and distrusts the impulse of the moment. He does not like excitement, takes matters of everyday life with proper seriousness and likes a well-ordered mode of life. He keeps his feelings under close control, seldom behaves in an aggressive manner and does not lose his temper easily. He is reliable, somewhat pessimistic and places great value on ethical standards. He may also exhibit neurotic tendencies.

Famous Characters

To fix the two types of personality in your mind it will probably be helpful to choose examples of some strongly introverted and extroverted characters from history and fiction. Among the introverts you could include Hamlet, Sherlock Holmes, Robespierre, John Stuart Mill, the March Hare, Faust, Don Quixote and Kant. Characteristic extroverts are Mr. Pickwick, Bulldog Drummond, Alexandre Dumas, Donald Duck, Sir Winston Churchill, Samuel Pepys and Falstaff.

We are not suggesting, of course, that everyone is either an out-and-out extrovert or out-and-out introvert. The

Above left: the extrovert. He likes fast cars, glamorous women, and enjoys an active sex life. Donald Duck and Churchill were extroverts. Above: the introvert. He prefers solitude and stability and keeps his feelings under control. Don Quixote and Sherlock Holmes were introverts. But most people have something of each tendency in them.

position is similar to that in intelligence testing. At one end of the scale you have the mental defective, at the other the genius, with the majority of people falling in between, possessing IQs between 90 and 110. In the same way most people can be placed somewhere in the middle area of the extroversion-introversion scale, being neither one thing nor the other.

Nevertheless, the extroversion-introversion concept is a highly valuable instrument in giving us an insight into why we—and others—behave in a certain way . . . the effects of drugs and alcohol . . . our sexual attitudes . . . even our political beliefs.

Studies suggest, for instance, that introverted children thrive better when given only praise while extroverted children are more highly motivated by blame. In the field of art, introverts tend to prefer older, tradi-

tional works, extroverts more modern, even futuristic, creations. A similar pattern emerges in poetry, with the extrovert enjoying the simple type of poem with a regular rhyming scheme and heavily-accented rhythm while the introvert prefers more complex poetry with an irregular rhyming scheme and less obvious rhythms.

The extrovert and introvert also have different attitudes to sex. Compared to introverts, extroverts can be expected to have intercourse more frequently with more different partners and in more positions; to indulge in more varied sexual behavior outside intercourse and in longer precoital love play, and to masturbate less than introverts (because of the availability of other sexual outlets). Female extroverts would have orgasm more frequently than introverts.

In an experiment with 50 photographs of young women, ranging from buxom nudes to skinny fashion models, extrovert men tended to prefer the buxom nudes with their Marilyn Monroe-Jayne Mansfield figures while introverts tended to prefer the fully clothed "nice" girls with much less clearly marked secondary sexual characteristics.

Extroverts also like sex jokes, introverts are less in favor of them. This

Phoebus Photo

is quite contrary to the theory of Freud for whom laughter and amusement are derived from the escape, in the harmless form of a joke, of repressed material which had been relegated to the unconscious. In the light of this theory it would be the introvert, releasing his "guilt," who should enjoy sex jokes most. In fact, experiments have repeatedly shown the opposite to be true. It is the extrovert, given to showing open delight in sexuality, who laughs the loudest.

Is there any physiological difference between introverts and extroverts? Well, it seems that there is and it is related to a particular property of the cortex (top layer) of the brain, often referred to as *arousal* although the man in the street would probably prefer the word *alertness.* The brain waves of extroverts reveal them to be, on the whole, less alert than introverts. Bound up with this is the ability of the extrovert to learn faster than the introvert but, in the end, remember less. When he is presented with new material the more alert introvert is busily consolidating or transferring this material into his long-term memory—a process which interferes with his ability to remember in the short term—possibly because the same cells or neurons are involved and cannot serve both purposes simultaneously.

In fact, one experiment showed that, tested almost immediately after a memory exercise, extroverts remembered almost twice as much as intro-

verts; after five minutes the two groups remembered about the same amount; but, after 24 hours, the introverts had reversed the position and remembered almost twice as much as the extroverts.

It is interesting to note that stimulant drugs, like caffeine and nicotine, increase cortical arousal and, hence, consolidation. No wonder, therefore, that students smoke and drink coffee when they are studying—and no wonder that extroverts smoke more and drink more coffee. They stand in greater need of arousal.

The opposite quality to arousal is *reactive inhibition.* Reactive inhibition may be defined as a tendency which works against some piece of behavior being repeated immediately. We can now understand the very obvious pressure on extroverts for novelty, for change, for alteration. For them, the regular, the usual, the ordinary, become anathema, and they search for new stimuli as well as strong stimuli.

Social Attitudes and Politics

In general, it may be said that what characterizes the extrovert most is to prefer action to thought whereas, to the typical introvert, thought is preferable to action. It follows from this that the introvert is more easily able to accept socialization, the rules and regulations we create to make living together simpler. Socialization largely involves the inhibition of action, the *forte* of the

Look at this picture for one minute. Cover it and recall what you saw. Write down only the number of items remembered. Test yourself again in five minutes, then sometime tomorrow. If the number of items remembered starts high and falls sharply, you are more likely to be an extrovert than an introvert.

gregarious extrovert.

In particular, the greater part of socialization may be said to consist of the erection of barriers to the immediate satisfaction of aggressive and sexual impulses. These barriers are absolutely essential if society is to survive. In some form they exist even in the most primitive type of society. Yet, however essential they may be to society, they are irksome and annoying to the individual who finds himself thwarted in the expression of what, to him, are perfectly natural desires and wishes.

Thus, here is a potential area of great conflict, and it is here, if anywhere, that we would expect the most marked contrast between the extrovert and introvert. How would this conflict tend to show itself in the field of social attitudes and political behavior?

Once again we can expect to find a scale ranging from an extremely introverted (over-socialized) type of attitude to an extremely extroverted (under-socialized) type of attitude. On the one side we would expect a strong insistence on barriers of one kind or another to the free expression of sexual and aggressive impulses. These barriers might be of a religious nature or an ethical nature, but they would all be aimed at restricting socially unacceptable behavior. We should find a regard for conventions and rules protecting society from some of the more biological drives of human nature.

Animal Instincts

On the other side of the scale we would expect the opposite—a relatively open demand for a relaxation of prohibitions, an overt desire for the direct expression of sexual and aggressive urges, and the denigration of religious and ethical standards felt to stand in the way. The extrovert would be tough-minded in his desire to override conventions and seek direct expression of the animal instincts of human nature.

In more concrete terms, *conservative* introverts tend toward religious attitudes and beliefs, *radical* introverts toward pacifistic and Quaker-type ideals. For their part, *conservative* extroverts will tend toward such attitudes as believing in the death penalty and flogging criminals and being against racial tolerance (he will consider colored people inferior) while the *radical* extrovert tends toward belief in companionate marriage, easier divorce laws and that Sunday observance is old-fashioned.

A similar alignment may be seen in the field of politics. If you are a conservative extrovert, you are quite likely to hold Fascist beliefs; if you are a radical extrovert, Communist beliefs.

The extroversion-introversion concept also gives us deeper insight into the effect of drugs and alcohol on different people and why some are more accident prone than others.

Take three people, A, B and C. B is an extrovert, C is an introvert, A is an average person. We can deduce that B, the extrovert, will have a low tolerance of depressant drugs like alcohol, which are known to have an extroverting effect; C, the introvert, will have a low tolerance of stimulant drugs like amphetamine or caffeine, which have an introverting effect; and A will respond more or less equally, and safely, to both types of drug, stimulant or depressant.

The Dangerous Extrovert

From this it can be seen that extroverts are potentially a greater danger than introverts on our roads. The extrovert is by nature inclined to drink and, because alcohol has an extroverting effect, he can quickly be pushed off the end of the extroversion-introversion scale. Furthermore, extroverts are more prone to involuntary rest pauses than are introverts. During an involuntary rest pause a driver is to all intents and purposes asleep and not paying attention to the task in hand. Alcohol, being an extroverting drug, has the effect of increasing the occurrence and prolonging such pauses. The person predisposed to accident proneness, in terms of his personality, is therefore also the person predisposed to increasing his accident proneness by drinking.

Such drivers, of course, are quite

unconscious of what is happening, and have no idea that they are becoming a danger to themselves and everybody else. They may be duped into thinking they are fit to drive because they can walk a chalk line or carry out similar simple tests. In fact, for the extreme extrovert, even the smallest amount of drink increases his chances of being involved in an accident because it increases his involuntary rest pauses, which he is not conscious of and has no means of assessing.

Finally, a further factor which makes such drivers a greater danger is that laboratory tests have proved that, given the chance to go fast and make many errors, or to go slow and make few errors, the extrovert who has been drinking plumps for speed and mistakes while the introvert who has been drinking plays it safe.

The basic accident proneness of the extrovert was demonstrated in an investigation into the human factor in flying accidents in South Africa. It was found that accident-prone pilots were significantly more extroverted, rather more emotional, panicked more easily, were more easily stimulated and therefore more distractible, that they tended to act on impulse and were generally less cautious, that their behavior was generally more variable and they were apt to be influenced by the mood of the moment.

To return briefly to the relevance of the extroversion-introversion concept to the function of drugs, criminal and psychopathic behavior tends to be found predominantly in extroverted persons. There are, of course, other

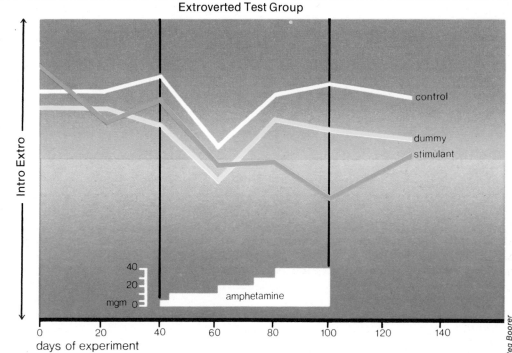

Extroverted Test Group

When stimulant drugs are given to extroverts their behavior becomes more introverted. The diagram shows what happened when a group of delinquents (all extroverts) were given amphetamine. The white and yellow lines show the behavior of a control group given no drugs and another group given dummy tablets. They remained in the red zone. However the green line indicates that this group, when given the maximum drugs — indicated by the blocked white area — moved significantly into the blue zone of introverted behavior. The scale at the foot of the diagram indicates the duration of the experiment. The introverted behavior of the test group continued for some time after drug administration ceased.

control

dummy

stimulant

Intro Extro

40
20
mgm 0
amphetamine

0   20   40   60   80   100   120   140
days of experiment

Reg Boorer

factors involved, such as inherited features of their nervous system. Nevertheless, as far as excessive extroversion is the fault, it should follow from the earlier example of A, B and C that some improvement should result from the administration of a stimulant drug designed to shift him in the direction of greater introversion.

Much of the early work in this connection was done with so-called behavior-disordered children. It was found, fairly uniformly, that stimulant drugs produced an immediate and, in some cases, almost miraculous effect. Children became much quieter, ceased to shout, became less excitable and more law-abiding. They also took in their lessons much better and, altogether, improved by something like 50 percent.

It was also demonstrated that if the opposite kind of drug was administered—a depressant, designed to make them even more extroverted—they became very much worse. This is interesting because, in the case of neurotics, who tend to be introverted people, barbiturates and other depressant drugs (which have an extroverting effect) are used medicinally nowadays to produce a quietening down of excessive fears.

Limitations

Extroversion and introversion are not the only terms in which personality can be analyzed. With many other investigators, however, we have found them the most important and most useful in describing human behavior.

Yet, although far more flexible and sophisticated than the Greeks' theory of the four humors, they are still not in themselves able to deal with all the complex factors that go to make up the human personality. We have said that criminals tend to be extroverts and neurotics tend to be introverts. Yet not by any means all extroverts tend to be criminals. Nor are by any means all introverts neurotic. Then, in the field of careers, you will find introverts happily involved in such diverse pursuits as the visual arts and the corridors of business power.

To explain these apparent discrepancies, we have to introduce another concept — emotionality. It acts as a drive which boosts and exaggerates the typical behavior of the extrovert (outgoing, pleasure-seeking, active) and the introvert (inward-turned, submissive). By applying it we can subdivide the extrovert and introvert into two further categories—the stable and the unstable.

A person's handwriting can say a great deal about him. It can tell us whether he is bold or shy, imaginative or dull, happy or sad.

However, nobody—least of all a responsible graphologist — would claim that this method of assessing personality was utterly reliable. But, at the same time, a close and expert examination of the way in which somebody writes often reveals an astonishingly accurate picture.

In psychological terms, handwriting is the outward expression of the inner individuality. And, broadly speaking, it is generally possible to tell if this individuality inclines towards extroversion or introversion.

The handwriting of an extrovert tends to be large and slants well forward. It is writing carried out quickly, running continuously to the right.

An introvert's handwriting is just the opposite: small, leans back and the slowness with which it is done emphasizes the leftwards strokes and tails.

The examples shown on this page are extremes of the two types and clearly demonstrate the main differences.

The first example, "Mr. John Gay," was written by a young, progressive American businessman. He is full of energy and enthusiasm and confidently dedicated towards high profits and rapid expansion. From his handwriting he would also appear to be an obvious extrovert.

But the second example, "I shall be interested to," denotes introversion. The person who wrote it is an 18-year-old boy. He lives in a remote country village with an overindulgent mother. He has no ambition, no self-confidence, he shrinks back from any personal contacts and is quite unable to make any decisions for himself.

When we examine these two examples more closely we learn how the assessments are made. The extrovert's handwriting ascends steadily across the page. This indicates an optimistic and buoyant outlook. The introvert's sinks back. However, unless the angle is excessive, this could merely mean that the writer is suffering from tiredness or ill-health. It does not necessarily have any psychological significance.

The large upper loops in the man's handwriting point to extroversion, while the short loops of the country boy show the opposite. The extrovert's handwriting flows smoothly across the page. But the introvert's is jerky, evidenced by the frequent breaking of words. The weak *t* crossings show introversion, as does the labored, stilted and indeterminate style. Another factor pointing to extroversion in the case of the American businessman is his unusual but ostentatious letter formations.

However, in spite of these apparent differences, they are not really sufficient to judge if a person is truly extrovert or introvert. Many handwriting styles combine the characteristics of both. They contradict each other, such as widely-spaced words containing narrow individual letters. This signifies outward normality in relationships and a degree of extroversion. But it also shows that the writer is suffering from an acute inner conflict—probably emotional.

Clearly, if anything like a proper character assessment is to be made through a person's handwriting, it is not enough to look at isolated examples. The whole writing pattern must be examined and other factors taken into account before a decision can be reached.

The Extrovert:
1. **Steeply ascending across the page.**
2. **Slanting well forward.**
3. **Large upper loops.**
4. **Original letter formations.**

The Introvert:
1. **Runs horizontally across the page.**
2. **Slants backwards.**
3. **Small upper loops.**
4. **Indeterminate *t* crossings.**

All you want to know about...

It can occur at any time. Suddenly, the unexpected happens and mind and body react. The mother at home sees her child endangered; a phone call shatters the businessman's carefully prepared plans. Stress comes into all our lives in hundreds of different ways. It can last a few moments or years. How can we recognize the symptoms? What can we do about it . . . if anything? Like any other emotion, the more we know about it the more we can control it. This series of questions and answers attempts to do just that.

Q **WHAT ARE THE PRINCIPAL CAUSES OF STRESS?**

A The answer here is–anything that pushes the body out of its "normal" pattern of activity. It's helpful here to see the body as a homeostatic system, that is to say one which keeps itself in a constant state of equilibrium. For example, if body temperature rises, one perspires to lose heat; if one's blood becomes short of oxygen, respiration picks up to supply more. The self-leveling mechanisms within the body act with considerable speed, but the system is also very highly tuned, and

when violent changes take place it may take some time to return to normal. It is when the threatening or unpleasant forces never allow the system to return to normal that the worst conditions of stress arise, and it is this kind of situation that most people are referring to when they talk about "the stress of life," "the rat race," etc. If we discount the short-term *stressors* for which it is easy to find a suitable adjusting response (if you prick your finger with a pin you pull your hand away!) and major assaults on the body by disease or illness, it is fairly clear that for modern man the principal causes of stress are psychological. It is these, for which there is no simple, short-term solution, no easy adjustment of the internal homeostat, which cause

the most trouble and which lie at the root of much of man's unhappiness.

WHAT IS STRESS?

Stress is a complex condition of body and mind caused by unusual or threatening situations in the external world, and persisting until these situations are removed. The condition may be short or long-term, and the causes or *stressors* may be predominantly either physiological or psychological, with the latter tending to be the more troublesome. All human beings, from birth to death, are subject to periodic bursts of stress. The reason for this is simple–we live in a dangerous and hostile world in which the unexpected is always likely to occur. In this threatening environment, when danger occurs it often does so with great speed, and for any animal to survive and replicate its species, it must be equipped with an enormously efficient and more or less totally automatic nervous system. When danger is detected by the body's remote sensing equipment, a state of "alert" is signaled, throwing the central nervous system out of its normal "ticking over" level into an emergency gear which prepares the creature for appropriate action to escape from the threatening situation. The alert state involves a number of major changes in the body's physiology and biochemistry which in turn lead to psychological sensations which we know of as "emotions." These may occasionally be pleasant, as in "love," but on the whole they tend to be unpleasant and drive the individual to change circumstances as quickly as he can. And here we come to the main point—it is the period *between the onset of the alerted condition,* whether this be psychological or physiological, *and the elimination of the threatening or annoying problems* which is known as a state of stress. Hence a baby, when hungry, is in a state of stress and will signal this by crying until food is brought. At different levels of life, a schoolboy faced with a difficult exam, a businessman caught in a traffic jam, an older person concerned about a forthcoming surgical operation, all find themselves in stress of varying degrees of intensity and significance. It is part of the price we pay for having a highly responsive nervous system, and for living in a challenging and generally surprising world.

HOW DOES AGE AFFECT STRESS?

In one way the older a person the less well equipped he is to deal with environmental and psychological stresses. His brain becomes less efficient at processing information and his body becomes less capable of responding to change. Undoubtedly increasing age

means that the stress load will be progressively harder to bear. Fortunately there is a counterbalancing force. As people get older they tend to be less ambitious and less inclined to take on responsibilities with which they cannot cope. As old age approaches domestic and financial problems also tend to have eased and the individual's more relaxed attitude to life means that he sets himself fewer and fewer goals which he suspects that he cannot achieve. The age group at the greatest risk from stress are those in the 35-50 bracket, when the flexibility and physical fitness of youth has begun to wane, and yet when career and financial challenges are at their most extreme. On the other hand, stress can also be seen in young children, typically when they are set goals not by themselves but by ambitious and dominating parents. Chronic stress of this kind can lead to severe problems in adolescence.

ARE WOMEN MORE PRONE TO STRESS THAN MEN?

The answer to this is both yes and no, for the question is not as simple as it sounds. The reason for this is that the biological differences between men and women and the social differences which also exist in contemporary society tend inevitably to push men and women into different lifestyles. Woman on the whole is groomed from the time she is a little girl towards a life of domesticity and child-bearing. Man, on the other hand, is cast in the role of the breadwinner and defender of house and home. For men and women therefore the life goals are qualitatively and quantitatively different. In most modern societies the greatest responsibilities in all but child-bearing rest with the male, and he is therefore usually more at risk from the point of view of stress. To the degree that he is successful in meeting his goals, so he will be free of stress. In the case of women most of the goals involve the bearing and raising of children and of course the same argument applies—to the degree that she is able to meet these goals, so she will be free from stress. However there is a joker in the pack. In recent years contraception has dramatically cut the size of most women's families, and while this may make an easier life in many respects, it introduces novel psychological and biological difficulties. Many psychologists now believe that woman's natural inclination towards child-bearing may conflict with her historically recent state of emancipation. For many women their basic drives may be channeled successfully into a professional life, but

others are not so fortunate. It is perhaps significant that the highest incidence of stress and its frequent psychoneurotic resultants in women are to be found among educated and affluent women with small families and few or no interests outside their home. Stress complaints are also typically associated with the menopause when women are obliged to face the fact that their child-bearing days are over. Stress situations of this kind will of course be greatly reduced when the role of women in our society is updated and more clearly defined.

ARE THERE DIFFERENT KINDS OF STRESS?

Yes, stress can be either short-term or long-term, and may have a physical or a psychological bias. Let us take duration first. Short-term stress is the kind of situation which arises when we are briefly startled or shocked by something—a loud noise, a sudden movement, a pain in the finger or whatever. These stress-states are mostly short-lived because corrective action is easily taken, generally automatically, by the body. Occasionally the *stressors* (it is important to distinguish between stress and the things that *cause* it) may be less physically based. For example, one may be shocked by an unpleasant remark made by a friend, or by a piece of bad news about the state of one's bank account. Again, corrective action of some kind, even if it's just a matter of "thinking over the problem" can be taken and the stress will vanish as solution is found. Unfortunately on the whole, psychological stressors are less easily dealt with than those with a physical base, and what is known as chronic stress can occur. Classically this is brought about by a sustained series of shocks or unpleasant events, or by remorseless psychological pressures such as major marital, economic or occupational worries. Stress of this kind is not easily removed and apart from its directly debilitating effect on the sufferer's mood and personality, the persistent physiological and biochemical changes which go hand in hand with it tend to build up and induce even longer-term side effects.

WHAT ARE THE COMMON SYMPTOMS OF STRESS?

There are few symptoms of short-term stress other than those which familiarly go hand-in-hand with an excited state of mind—a racing pulse, a feeling of "butterflies" in the stomach and a general sense of mental sharpness. Long-term stress, as might be expected, will produce more enduring symptoms which range on a sliding scale of severity from a general feeling of anxiety (often without being able to ascribe a cause to it), sleeplessness, inability to concentrate, general unsociability and irritability, to chronic dyspepsia (indigestion), high blood pressure and, at the very worst, stomach ulcers and heart trouble. Of course it can't be too heavily emphasized that these are some common symptoms of severe stress, but are not invariably associated with it. Equally these symptoms may denote some other physical condition and medical advice should always be sought when problems of this kind persist. Occasionally prolonged stress, particularly when the individual is not aware that he is suffering from it, may lead to symptoms which appear to have no direct relationship to any stress condition. Classically these symptoms include many phobias, memory problems and difficulties with interpersonal relationships.

CAN STRESS BE CAUSED BY "OVERWORK"?

It depends on what is meant by overwork. If one's talking about *too much* work, then the answer is "Yes," for overwork in this sense is itself an indication that one is unable to solve one's work problems. It might also be because the problem is of a fundamentally different kind—for example one may have to overwork because it is the only way to

get enough money to get oneself out of debt. In such circumstances one has not only the stress-inducing problem which is causing one to slave for hour after hour, but also the steady build-up of fatigue and anxiety which must follow. When most people ask this question, however, they're generally thinking of *hard work*—the kind that will envelop a student studying for his exams, a musician rehearsing for a concert, a businessman getting his enterprise off the ground, an author hurrying to finish a book by a deadline, etc. The fact is that hard work of this kind—which is generally concerned with setting a series of goals and achieving them by one means or another—is very rarely stressful, for the system is only under stress intermittently. In fact, contrary to popular belief, the hard-working, go-getting type (provided that he never sets psychological or physical goals beyond his reach) will generally live through his life in a less stressful state than the slower, more indecisive individual whose relative failure to achieve even the limited goals he sets himself may place him in a constant state of dissatisfaction and thus make him prone to mental stress.

CAN STRESS BRING ON A HEART ATTACK?

Yes, though short-term stress of the "sudden shock" variety is very unlikely to do so unless there is a heart weakness or disease. Long-term stress exercises its dire effects in a number of ways. To understand this one must remember that the point about stress is that it occurs in the period between the body's initial response to a threatening or unpleasant situation and the removal or eradication of the situation. To say that a person is chronically frustrated in his job—perhaps he is attempting to cope with an economically ailing business, working alongside unfriendly associates, or for a demanding or unsympathetic boss—is to say that he is in a more or less constant state of stress. His body and mind are persistently alerted by the unpleasant job situation and yet he is for one reason or another quite unable to correct matters. Thus the alerting reactions, both psychological and physiological, are maintained and in due course major changes in the body and its organs take place. A number of long-term changes may occur, but the one most likely to induce spectacular and sudden death is related to a high level of cholesterol or fatty acid in the blood. Cholesterol is an essentially life-giving substance, pumped into the blood stream at a high level by the adrenal

glands when a stressful situation arises. A violent burst of activity on the part of the individual will cause the fatty acids to be used up and the system will return to normal. Constant stress of a psychological kind however, maintains a high cholesterol level and when this is not reduced by physical exercise, the fatty acids are deposited on the walls of the arteries. This in turn leads to high blood pressure. The constantly stressed individual is therefore slowly impairing the circulation of blood in his body and thus during a sudden and major emergency, the constricted arteries may deprive the heart of blood and induce a coronary with fatal consequences.

ARE FAT PEOPLE LESS PRONE TO STRESS?

There is an old wives' tale that fat people are generally good-natured and jovial, and like many other tales in its class, it has some vague measure of scientific support. Thirty years ago the American psychologist Sheldon classified people into three main body types—endomorphs (fat), mesomorphs (muscular) and ectomorphs (thin). The endomorphs he considered to be generally easy-going and good-natured, but his theory has been subject to much critical assault. Possibly there are biochemical differences and peculiarities which make the fat person somewhat less adventurous and therefore unlikely to set up physical or psychological goals which he cannot achieve. But this is not the whole story. Many excessively fat people are compulsive eaters and are particularly prone to eating bouts when depressed or anxious. In many cases this excessive eating is a response to chronic stress which it somehow helps to alleviate. In that sense therefore since the highly obese person is free from stress as long as he or she can continue eating, then one could say that fat people are less prone to stress. It is a dubious argument however, for the obsessive eating would not have arisen had not some degree of stress been present in the first place.

How many people are you?

Everyone has a different impression of the same person. A man's secretary sees him in one way, his wife another. And his own idea of himself is different again. This is called our sense of self and much depends on coming to terms with it. Starting in childhood, it develops through adolescence and establishes itself when we are adults.

A group of students once played an elaborate joke on a dull and unattractive girl. The results were far from what they expected.

They pretended they thought her extremely attractive and popular. And she believed them. Their attentions gave her a different idea of herself as others saw her. She now believed she was someone people liked. Her "self-concept," as some psychologists term it, gradually changed, so that after some months she was relaxed and confident, lost her dullness and became, in fact, attractive and popular.

From early childhood, every person develops an idea of what he himself is like—his physical appearance, his ability and aptitudes, and his likability. This self-concept will strongly affect his behavior throughout life, influencing his degree of success in all sorts of relationships.

Sense of Self

A baby's self-concept comes gradually. Its first movements are efforts to explore and handle parts of its own body. Slowly it discovers the existence of itself as a separate entity—separate from the people and objects that surround it. While it can feel pain and sensation, it cannot locate them in its body. Sometime between the ages of 12 and 18 months, the child will be able to recognize its own reflection in a mirror—it has, then, learned to look at itself.

Psychological self-concept is a later development, but emerges in rather the same way as the physical self-concept. A child observes his own behavior and other people's reactions to it. His opinion of himself will develop in accordance to the amount of admiration or censure his behavior variously receives. A great deal too much of one or the other will give him an unrealistic self-concept

and tend to make him so vulnerable or resentful that it may impede his development.

As he realizes that he does not have the same effect on each person, a child has to learn to adapt his self-concept to fit these bewilderingly different reactions. He will form an idea of himself as either attractive or unattractive, according to different people's expectations of him: mother, father, brothers or sisters; then other children, then teachers and, eventually, sexual partners, employers and colleagues and spouse and offspring.

Shocks to one's self-concept are common and inevitable. One such shock occurs when a child first goes to school. If his parents were overprotective of him and gave him too rosy an idea of himself, he will experience a sudden shock when he has to measure his abilities against those of other children. Each change in environment may bring similar blows.

Great shocks to a person's self-concept—like someone he loves accusing him falsely of theft—may have a profoundly disturbing effect, and even persuade him to shape his life to fit the concept that particular person seems to have of him. Certainly if a child is continually blamed or denigrated, he will tend to devalue himself and act accordingly.

This was shown in a study of the relationship between parents' attitudes and their children's self-appraisals. The self-concepts of 75 delinquent boys were evaluated. Those boys whose parents often rejected them considered themselves inferior and inadequate. Those with mothers who were unstable and highly critical generally had a sense of themselves as bad and guilty. It is clear that the demoralized self-concepts of these boys were strongly influenced by the negative opinions

of their parents, and contributed to their delinquency.

Negative opinions of him will also hold back a child at school. Studies have shown that a teacher's expectations of a child will affect both his own actions and the responsiveness of the child. If the teacher measures his pupils by their clothes and manners and social background, he will assume the typical lower class child to be dull and unwilling, and the more middle class child to be bright and willing. The children will respond accordingly, the "dull" ones "opting out" in self-defense, and the "bright" ones becoming brighter.

As Others See Us

The effect of criticism of an individual's self-concept will vary widely not only because of variations of personality but as a result of what he has been conditioned to expect. Maternal "rejection," for instance, is commonly accepted in the British middle classes, where the child is usually sent away to a boarding school at an early age. Individual children may consequently feel rejected by their parents, but most will come to regard it in the same way society does

These five characters are studies in human personality, portraits of the many kinds of people we can be in a variety of situations. At the bottom is a man as he really is, but the other four figures circling around him show him in entirely different lights. Beginning at the lower left is the way his secretary sees him with a lecherous grin. That noble, manly visage is how he imagines himself and the bland, unprepossessing creature is his wife's perception. Last, downtrodden and ineffectual, is how he *feels* after confronting his boss.

Ron Embleton

—not as rejection, but as a mark of success. Therefore the child's self-concept is rather enhanced. Similarly, such children are expected to have sufficient confidence to respond positively when criticized—to be stung to higher achievement; lower class children are more likely to accede to the implied poor image of themselves.

Positive opinions can similarly transform someone's self-concept. Occasionally an intelligent child from a culturally deprived background may be seen as promising by a perceptive teacher. Encouragement will enable him to revise his concept of himself as an intellectually able person. With encouragement and effort he will be able to benefit from his education.

Identity and Adolescence

A small child's sense of self allows him to be aware of other people only in relation to himself. If a boy has a brother, he will be able to tell you that he has a brother, but will deny that his *brother* also has a brother. By the time he reaches puberty, he is more acutely aware of other people's reactions to his own self. He has to reorganize his image of his place in the world. The adolescent's task of discovering his identity is made all the more difficult by the rapid physical changes he is experiencing.

Because of their preoccupation with bodily changes, adolescents are quick to seize on physical characteristics as a means of evaluating each other. They are obsessed with physical appearance—boys now as absorbed as girls have been taught to be. Both will try out different roles and identities, different expressions, poses and gestures. Each will form an idea of the person he would like to be, and tends to hero-worship someone he feels has achieved this—someone known to him or, more often, some celebrity or a character in a book. He may adopt the mannerisms and speech of his chosen hero.

It is significant that many adolescent girls find it very difficult to extract admirable *heroines* from a favorite book, on which to model themselves. Like boys, they may choose a hero rather than a heroine. This is not necessarily because they want to change sex (although studies

A young woman ponders as she walks with her husband. Many marriages fail because some men try too hard to live up to an impossible standard of masculinity and dominance set by society and still accepted by some women today.

Marshall Cavendish

show that many girls would prefer to be boys, whereas hardly any boy would admit the reverse). It is simply that women in fiction are usually portrayed in insipid secondary or domestic roles and are allowed very little character at all: there is very little for a spirited adolescent to admire and imitate.

Eventually the adolescent should formulate a fairly stable idea of the sort of person he would like to be. The goals he sets must be reasonable, obtainable ones—or he will ultimately begin to devalue himself.

An additional hazard for the adolescent in our society is that his "crisis of identity" may be delayed for a long time by higher education. This makes the adjustment accordingly all the more arduous.

In fact, our urban industrial society makes the adolescent identity crisis peculiarly difficult. In less-advanced societies, present and past, self-concept was probably much simpler and far less powerful in its effects than now: people's roles in life were standardized, so that each person knew more or less from the beginning of his life what was expected of him. There was comparatively little scope for variation of life style, occupation, or roles within relationships. A person was also more likely to have a firmer corporate identity—as a part of a group. In fact, he would be less "self" conscious, and less isolated.

Sexual Role-playing

In contrast, an urban industrial society offers a great variety of roles and opportunities. Even where someone is born into a category that is traditionally given a strongly limited role—lower class, or female, or black—there are so many manifest and increasing exceptions to the rules that a growing number of such people successfully rebel against these arbitrary limits.

The complex hierarchy of our society, and its affluence, make self-concept a painfully complex affair for most people: we have so many types of success to measure ourselves against, and so many desirable, image-evoking consumer goods held up to us by advertising.

In a simple or primitive society, the "gender" self-concepts we encourage boys and girls to acquire would be more appropriate. In primitive societies the male had a clear masculine role to perform: hunting or fighting, for instance; and the female would spend a greater part of her life childbearing (the life span was usually very

BRAVE, STRONG AND MANLY **CHINS** WEAK AND SPINELESS

LEVEL-HEADED AND LOGICAL **EARS** SLOW, STUPID AND CLUMSY

HONEST AND FORTHRIGHT **EYES** DEVIOUS AND SHIFTY

EASYGOING, GOOD-HUMORED **NOSES** PARSIMONIOUS AND CRABBY

INTELLIGENT, CULTURED **BROWS** THICK AND UNCIVILIZED

GENEROUS AND WARM **MOUTHS** SOUR, MEAN AND CRITICAL

Quartet

We know that looks play an important part in molding a self-concept; we often begin to regard ourselves as others do, their perceptions becoming self-fulfilling. This is often unfortunate, because a person's physical characteristics, in the beginning at least, do not necessarily indicate his feelings or his abilities. Yet while small eyes do not signal an inherent shiftiness, a person who has them may feel the conditioned distrust of others and so avoid their glance, confirming the impression that he is not straightforward or honest. Similarly, someone who has the face of a "dullard" may begin to act like one no matter how intelligent he is. On the other hand, the demands placed on a man with a stalwart jaw may be just as hard to bear: he could be a hopeless coward; still (luckily for the beautiful people) his looks could give him confidence and courage. But woe to the man who is attracted to a girl with a warm and generous face—and a cold heart!

short for both of them). And if a man happened to be particularly incompetent in his allotted masculine role, he would probably be put out of the running by being wounded or killed.

A common difficulty in marriage is that the woman has usually been conditioned to believe that her husband will be a competent and dominant creature, and she has anticipated being looked after. Since he is only human, and an individual, he is very unlikely to be competent in all the areas labeled "masculine" in our society. But, because he too has been conditioned to believe in the "masculine" role, he will almost certainly lay claim to the role, no matter how badly he performs parts of it. Such is our conditioning that they are both deeply embarrassed by instances of poor performance.

Their difficulty is to reconcile their unreal expectations of each other.

Numbers of men are glad to encourage a full and individual self-concept in their wives, and some men and women have sufficiently well developed self-concepts not to need to play at the stereotyped roles of the competent husband and dependent wife.

A group of university students were given questionnaires to find out what they thought typical males and females were like, and also what they themselves were like. The results showed a strong agreement between the sexes about the differences between men and women. Moreover, typically male characteristics were valued more highly than typically female ones. In addition, the self-concepts of males and females were seen to be remarkably similar to those which described their respective stereotypes. From this study it seems that females tend to have a negative value of their own worth when compared to males.

Self-concept of one's self in gender terms is probably more important thar any other single area of life, since our happiness depends so much on our enjoyment of personal relationships in our leisure time. But it is one in which we are so strongly conditioned that it is difficult to adapt to reality.

Know Yourself

Fortunately our ability to adapt our self-concept never diminishes. It can improve at any time, with the right stimulus. But it is also necessary to recognize our ability for self-deception. This applies even to our physical self-image. Since our appearance can be checked in mirrors, there should be little scope for self-deceit here. But in fact most people automatically *pose* when they are about to look in a mirror—they stand more upright than usual, perhaps, or pat their hair into place or tilt their head to a flattering angle. This is so unconsciously done that people rarely see their reflection *un*posed. Most people have at some time experienced shock in a street or shop by catching sight of an almost unrecognizable self, unexpectedly reflected in a mirror or shop window. Unposed, one suddenly sees oneself as others see one. If the average psychological concept of self is as inaccurate as that, perhaps it is as well that there is as yet no way of coming face to face with an uncontrovertibly accurate reflection of it.

A young couple face the future together. The chances of their staying together may depend on each having a realistic concept of the other's true role in marriage.

It is interesting to note that fathers are typically much more concerned about appropriate sex roles than are mothers. They exert considerable pressure on their sons to adopt masculine patterns of behavior although they are not as demanding of their daughters. Consequently, boys are generally aware of sex differences much earlier than girls are. They are also more reluctant to deviate from these socially defined roles.

Since society allots him the more positive role, this reconciliation usually takes place by the wife pretending that he is competent. Studies have shown, in fact, that a high proportion of the people who described their marriage as "successful" were doing just this. "Success" was claimed where the wife agreed with her husband's self-concept—no matter how unreal that was—and was not affected by whether or not he agreed with his wife's self-concept. That is, as long as she would agree that he was what he claimed to be, all was well; but the importance of *her* self-concept was dismissed by both of them. (Such studies do not, of course, follow the course of such marriages, so we do not know how long these deceptive relationships survived.)

Hopefully this is slowly changing.

Marshall Cavendish

Improve your thinking

Is your thinking efficient? We all think, even if we are not philosophers; everyday life demands it, in balancing a budget or making out a map route or arranging furniture in a room. We have all followed an argument, some- times spotted flaws in it, wrestled with problems. Most of us like to sharpen our wits with card games or cross- word puzzles. But we all know that our performance could be improved.

It is important to realize that "think- ing" is not just one kind of activity and different people think in different ways. Are you a visualizer? Do you "see" numbers or days of the week in different colors? All these prob- lems are based on visual patterns; if you solve them right away, without using words, you are probably artistic and imaginative, with a good memory for images. If you work them out logically, step-by-step, then reason- ing rather than intuition is your forte.

Questions

PUZZLE 1: Find the next pattern in the series from the four above.
PUZZLE 2: Which is the odd man out?
PUZZLE 3: Using a pencil, trace the most direct route from start to finish.
PUZZLE 4: Find the missing patterns in the series, choosing from the shapes on the right.

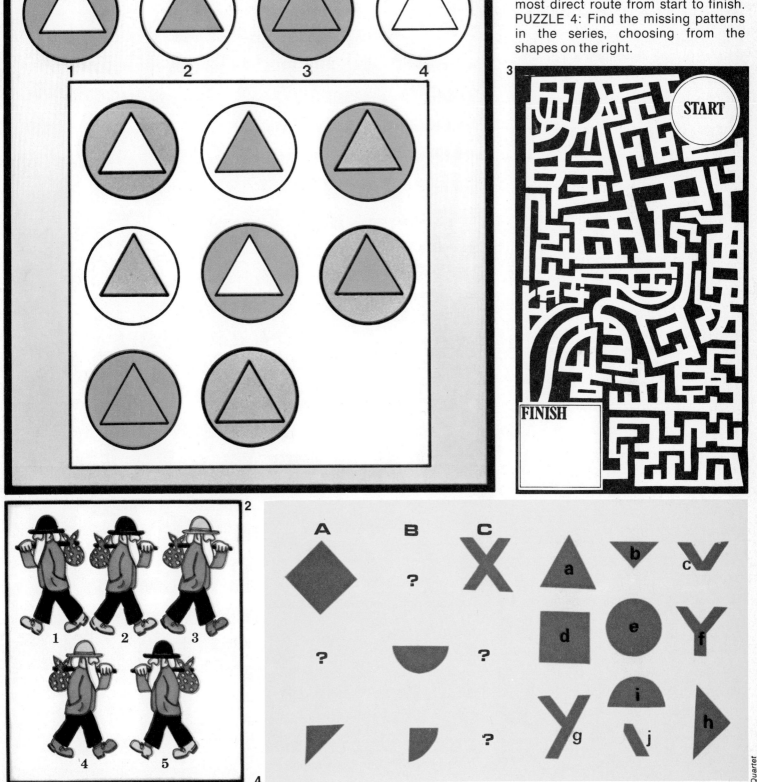

Answers

PUZZLE 1 **No. 4** (each series has an outer circle and inner triangle of each color).

This problem is based on sequence, and involves both the ability to visualize and logical thought. How did you arrive at your answer? A good ''guess'' could mean very fast thought processing. Were you willing to risk a guess, or did you want to be sure of the right answer before making a choice?

PUZZLE 2 **No. 2** (note that figures 1 and 5 are identical, so are figures 3 and 4).

Like puzzle 1, this can be solved step-by-step or by following a ''hunch'' that one figure *looked* odd.

PUZZLE 3 How many false moves did you make?

This maze involves good ''orientation''; men usually perform better than women. Good driving and understanding machines involves orientation. If you can solve this problem easily, you have a good ''sense of direction.'' If you find it difficult, you may not be attending to the most important clues, but trying to take in too much information at once.

PUZZLE 4 **A – (h)**
 B – (e)
 C – (c), (j)

If you get the right answers, can you say *why*? Each line of the puzzle has a whole figure, half of that figure and a quarter of the figure. Some people work this out, then make a choice; others ''see'' the answer without knowing *why*.

4 CORRECT Your visual and logical ability is high. If you ''guessed'' you are an intuitive thinker.
3 CORRECT Visual and logical ability above average.
2 CORRECT A good average score; you are probably an all-round thinker.
1 CORRECT Visual thinking is not your strongest point. You may need more practice in attending to visual pattern, or you may think mainly with words.
NONE CORRECT Did you give yourself a chance? Perhaps you guessed too quickly or were distracted as you worked. You may think in nonvisual terms and prefer to use words or actions.

Even if you worked out all four successfully, you can improve the speed and techniques of your thinking. If you found some or all of them impossible, practice and insight into your own strengths and weaknesses will lead to much better performance. Try to notice how you think in everyday life. Are you dreamy or precise, do you play safe or take risks by guessing? There is a place for different approaches; the secret is to know which is best for the problem in hand. Most problems yield to a number of different methods, and you can make the most of the skills you possess and acquire ones you do not.

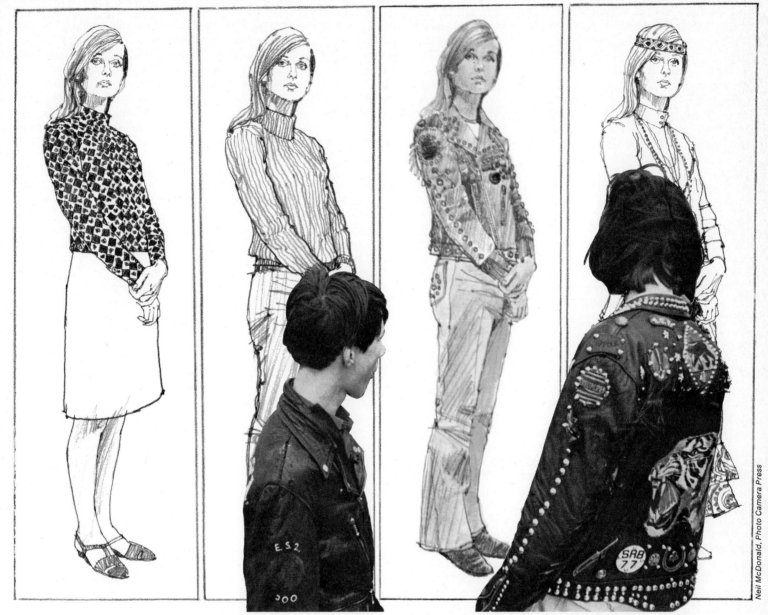

Neil McDonald, Photo Camera Press

A matter of looks

Do you consider yourself physically attractive to the opposite sex? How important are looks in determining choice of a marriage partner? And do we deliberately create an image of ourselves to make us more attractive to a particular person, as the picture above suggests?

Most of us want to be thought physically attractive by the opposite sex and both men and women go to great lengths to improve their beauty. But does it really matter? Do we worry overmuch about how we look? In adolescence the answer to both questions is an emphatic "Yes!"

When the two psychologists Ellen Berscheid and Elaine Walster carried out a series of college-level studies on blind dates, they discovered that intelligence and personality were unimportant in the students' assessments of how much they liked their dates. Physical attractiveness, pure and simple, was all that mattered. This was expanded in a further study by psychologist Karen Dion. She found that students considered good looking people to be generally more sensitive, kinder, more interesting and sexually more responsive than less attractive persons.

Attracting a Mate

Looks are also significant in determining our choice of a marriage partner. There is clear evidence that people tend to marry someone who is rated by outside observers at a similar level of attractiveness as themselves. Where there is a notable discrepancy between a married couple, the less attractive one probably offers some compensation such as social status, wealth or physical skill.

A study by psychologists Tony Brazendale and Glenn Wilson suggests that our perception of ourselves as attractive or unattractive has a distinct influence on our personality.

A group of 97 female student teachers filled out a questionnaire rating their enjoyment of a series of

42 risqué picture postcards. The sexual attractiveness of each of the girls was rated without their knowledge by two lecturers from a different university who did not know any of them personally. The results showed a tendency for the unattractive girls to be inhibited, puritanical and opposed to sexual freedom. They preferred cartoons which depicted sexually attractive girls as the center of lecherous male attention. Apparently plain girls try to protect themselves against awareness of their disadvantage by adopting puritan attitudes, but at the same time enjoy fantasies about male advances.

Sex Objects

When this research was reported in the press, the authors were bombarded by angry letters from all over the world. The writers protested that the study was trivial or provocative, that it had not been properly conducted, or that it should never have been carried out in the first place. Many of the letters were written by severely disturbed people, but the most coherent criticism was that it was impossible to measure attractiveness because everyone's taste is different. However, although people do vary as to what exactly catches their eye, the fact remains that there is a great deal of agreement among men as to which women are the most attractive. Beauty is not entirely a matter of personal preference. The outraged reaction to this research suggested that it had touched a highly emotional and taboo area and only serves to reinforce the belief in its psychological significance.

Members of the Women's Liberation Movement and certain religious organizations were disturbed because they felt that people were being treated as sex objects; which, of course, they were, for people are at least partially sex objects. Of course they are a lot of other things as well, but a scientist must focus all his attention on the specific area he is studying in order to make any headway. Thus it is sometimes useful to view the human brain as a computer, but this does not imply any devaluation of its unique non-mechanical characteristics.

Sexual attraction has a firm biological basis. It is dependent on the physical differences that have evolved between male and female. To some extent these differences are based on the original functions of men and women (man the hunter, woman the childbearer and nurse), but they have also developed to maximize sexual attraction, and particularly the

appeal of woman to man. This has recently been questioned by some psychologists taking an extreme position. They claim that sexual attraction is based entirely on propaganda and advertising. They ignore the fact that to be successful any exploitation must capitalize on an existing basic need.

Sex drive is based on hormones circulating in the blood. These have their major effect shortly after birth or possibly even in the prenatal period, during which they modify the structure of the brain long before any sex-role learning has taken place. After this critical period of brain development, the hormone balance is of relatively little importance. Because of this it is extremely difficult to alter the intensity or direction of an adult's sex drive by giving special hormone injections.

The incidence of homosexuality which, according to the Kinsey Report, may be as much as four percent of the population, does not disprove the biological basis of sex drive. For although a certain amount of homosexual behavior will occur in situations where the opposite sex is unavailable, such as in prisons and boarding schools, real homosexuals suffer from a male and female hormone deficiency.

Given that sexual attraction is usually based on the differences between the sexes, it follows that the points of maximum difference will be the most attractive and rousing. This means that, within certain limits, the more exaggerated these differences are, the more sexually attractive they will tend to be.

Woman, the Seducer

The idea behind make-up and beauty treatment is to emphasize some of the ways—fuller lips, narrower eyebrows, a softer complexion and the absence of facial hair—in which the female face is different from the male. Large breasts are normally seen as attractive up to the point where they lose firmness and begin to droop. The narrow waist and relatively broad hips are also major sexual stimuli. Most of these features are biologically based, but others are socially determined. For instance we regard long fingernails as a sexy feminine characteristic, even though, without cutting, a man's nails would grow just as long.

Desmond Morris, the anthropologist, has argued very plausibly that the strongest sexual stimulus the female human could use to attract a man

would be to bend over and push out her backside like an ape. He points out that enlarged buttocks are unique to the human female and represent a permanent equivalent of the swelling that occurs during ovulation (heat) in other primates. This is consistent with the fact that human females are sexually receptive throughout their cycle, whereas other animals are not.

Personality and Sexual Attraction

Morris goes on to argue that other parts of the female body that appear as "paired, fleshy hemispheres" work as "genital echoes," giving rise to an amount of sexual arousal which is dependent on the extent to which they are reminiscent of the primary sexual zone. These copies include the lips, shoulders and knees (all of which are sometimes recognized as having erotic significance) and most important the breasts. He points out that the human female is again unique among primates in having breasts which protrude even when she is not producing milk. Therefore he suggests that they must be pseudo-buttocks which serve to arouse men during face-to-face contact. To support this argument, Morris cites a variety of observations, for example that the tendency with women's clothes has been to improve the pseudo-buttock appearance of the breasts by pushing them upwards. They then become more bulging, rounder and closer together, making their cleavage more like buttocks.

Why resort to echoes at all? Presumably because the primary stimulus, the pudendum, which is after all what ultimately attracts men, is just too arousing to be displayed to any passing male. Civilized society could scarcely be maintained if sexual invitations were so explicit.

Although there is a great deal of agreement among men as to which women are the most attractive, there are obviously some individual differences. One interesting study of personality in relation to sexual preferences was conducted by Alvin Scodel at the University of Ohio. He tested Freud's idea that strongly dependent men would prefer women with large breasts. The results were significantly different, for dependent men actually tended to prefer small

Two men who are almost exactly opposite in appearance are shown at right. The man on the left gives an illustration of what men imagine women admire and the man on the right shows what women really admire.

WHAT MEN IMAGINE WOMEN ADMIRE (left)	%
Muscular chest and shoulders	21
Muscular arms	18
Penis (as suggested by tight trousers)	15
Tallness	13
Flat stomach	9
Slimness	7
Hair (texture, not length)	4
Buttocks	4
Eyes	4
Long legs	3
Neck	2

WHAT WOMEN REALLY ADMIRE (right)	%
Buttocks (usually described by women as "small and sexy")	39
Slimness	15
Flat stomach	13
Eyes	11
Long legs	6
Tallness	5
Hair	5
Neck	3
Penis	2
Muscular chest and shoulders	1
Muscular arms	0

Sunday Times

breasts. The Freudian theory that we should be most attracted to people who resemble our opposite sex parent is also unproven.

Jerry Wiggins and his colleagues at the University of Illinois set out to test the popular belief that men can be classified into three groups, breast men, leg men, or buttocks men, depending on the part of the female body they most liked. They asked a group of 95 students to rate a series of nude female silhouettes, which varied in the three body parts. The students also filled in a questionnaire so that their personality and details such as family background, hobbies and career intentions could be assessed and related to ratings.

Leg Men and Extroversion

The results confirmed that men could be classified according to the part of the female body with which they were most preoccupied. In addition they discovered some interesting relationships between these parts and the men's personalities and social backgrounds. Men who liked large-breasted women tended to be smokers, sportsmen, readers of *Playboy* and frequent daters. They were extrovert and masculine in their tastes. By contrast, men who preferred small breasts drank very little, were uninterested in sports, held conventional religious beliefs, were mildly depressed and submissive.

Men who liked large buttocks were characterized by a need for order, passivity and self-abasement, whereas men who liked small buttocks tended to be less dependent on organization and more self-confident. Men who liked large legs abstained from alcohol, were submissive, self-abasing and inhibited in social situations, but men who preferred small legs were more extrovert and exhibitionist. Preference for a large figure overall was associated with a high need for achievement and a high consumption of alcohol; those who preferred a small figure were more secure and less reliant on the trappings of achievement. Still further research along these lines should prove useful in understanding our individual differences in what we tend to see as attractive.

Effects of Nakedness

Professor Hans Eysenck and his colleagues in Britain have also studied the effect that personality differences have on physical preferences. Their main finding was that extroverts prefer women with large breasts and

Marshall Cavendish

A young couple in love. They have health and good looks, two qualities which count in mutual attraction.

buttocks, while introverts like smaller women. This is generally consistent with Wiggins's findings. The introverts also favored more fully-dressed women than the extroverts. Eysenck suggests that introverts tend to feel overwhelmed by naked or well-developed females, but usually feel more at ease with the thin and thoughtful type of woman.

How to Please a Woman

Andrew Mathews of Oxford University studied the reactions of 75 men to a series of pictures of women taken from various magazines. Some were from women's magazines and others from male-orientated girlie magazines. A third of the women were fully clothed, a third partially dressed, and a third completely naked. In line with previous findings there was some agreement among the men as to which women were the most sexually attractive. Those most desirable were

described as sexually inviting, graceful, young, or slender, whereas the less desirable ones were regularly described as prostitutes, vulgar, old and gross. But there were also significant individual differences. Manual workers tended to like conventionally well-dressed women rather than the trendy ones, while a group of homosexuals preferred the less threatening women. When the men were asked which of the women they would favor as long-term mates, they chose the ones who were elegantly attractive, and paid less attention to the sexy, provocative poses.

Whereas the features of women that are attractive to men are fairly widely recognized, there is more of a mystery concerning the physical characteristics of men that are sexually attractive to women. On the whole women are less concerned about physical attractiveness in men, or, rather, their basis of judgement is more complex and variable. Contrary to the popular male conviction, women are seldom interested in the size of his penis, whether he is circumcized or not, or the flexed diameter of his biceps.

Many women even claim to be disgusted by rippling muscles and cite small buttocks as the attribute they most admire in men. Other attractive features in men according to women are tallness, slimness (especially a flat stomach) and the eyes, where an intelligent or sexy expression matters more than their shape or color.

Cultural Influences

To some extent our judgement of physical attractiveness is influenced by cultural standards of beauty. Anthropologists claim that there is no universal agreement as to what constitutes attractiveness. The best known examples of cultural variation are the Arab preferences for plump women, and the liking for drooping or pendulous breasts in certain primitive tribes. But these exceptional cases should not blind us to the existence of valid generalizations. Instead they should be viewed as extremes of the variation which is always present, whether between different cultures or between different individuals within the same culture.

Wealth...

Explanations for these variances may be found in other characteristics with which the attractive physical quality in question is often associated. For example, in our culture we value a suntan partly because it indicates that one has been on a skiing or tropical holiday which imparts prestige. Similarly plumpness may be valued because of its associations with maternity or sumptuous living, and therefore wealth. Although the detailed aspects of what is considered beautiful may vary from society to society, one idea is universal. In every culture the woman's beauty plays a more important part in her overall attractiveness than the man's good looks do in his.

... and Health

One of the most important elements in attractiveness is apparent healthiness. People who are constantly complaining of ill health seldom seem sexy, however much they may evoke a maternal or protective response. This is possibly the reason we place such stress on clear skin, since skin tone is an excellent indicator of a person's state of health. We are also attracted to people who have a general zest for life. Drive, creativity, curiosity and sexual interest are all related qualities which are vital to our sexual attractiveness.

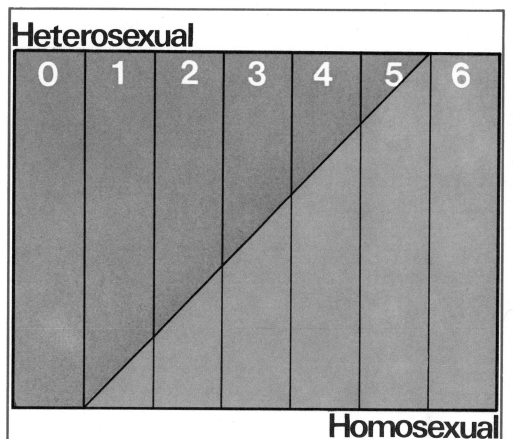

Most men assume that they are attracted exclusively to women. But facts, according to Kinsey, say otherwise. The average male can be both mentally and physically drawn to other men without being aware of the reaction.

The Kinsey homosexual-heterosexual rating scale

Kinsey not only found that 4 percent of the male population was permanently and exclusively homosexual (i.e. rate a 6 on the scale) but he also established the percentage of all males between the ages of 16 and 55 who featured on the scale in varying degrees for at least a 3-year period. Some 30 percent have had at least occasional homosexual experiences (i.e. rate 1-6), while a further 25 percent have more than occasional homosexual experiences (i.e. rate 2-6). Another 18 percent have at least as much of the homosexual as the heterosexual in their histories (i.e. rate 3-6), and 13 percent have more (i.e. rate 4-6). On the higher end of the scale, 10 percent are more or less exclusively homosexual (i.e. rate 5 or 6) whereas the final 8 per-

cent are exclusively homosexual.

These ratings have a dual basis. They take into account both a man's overt physical experience and his mental reactions, which may not necessarily be the same.

0s have no male physical contacts which result in erotic arousal and make no mental sexual response to people of their own sex.

1s have only occasional homosexual contacts involving physical or mental response.

2s have homosexual experiences which are more than occasional and respond positively to homosexual stimuli.

3s stand midway on the scale. They are about equally homosexual and heterosexual in their physical experience or mental reactions.

4s have more physical experience or mental reactions in the homosexual sphere, but maintain a fair amount of heterosexual activity, and still respond to heterosexual stimuli.

5s are almost exclusively homosexual both in their activities and reactions.

6s are exclusively homosexual both in terms of their physical experience and their mental reactions.

Keystone Press

Kinsey: Confession was good for the poll

More than 20 years ago an obscure American expert on insects, Dr. Alfred Kinsey, startled the world with a report on the sex habits of a generation. Today his name is still synonymous with sexual revelation although his intentions were purely scientific.

Dr. Alfred Kinsey's two volumes, *Sexual Behavior in the Human Male* and *Sexual Behavior in the Human Female*, commonly known as The Kinsey Report, caused a furor when published in 1948 and 1952. No doubt the effect today would be a lot less dramatic, although some of the report's revelations would probably still raise a permissive eyebrow.

The fact that questions about homosexual behavior and human sexual relations with animals were a perfectly routine part of every interview says a great deal about the answers Kinsey was receiving early in his research. In fact, after conducting his first 733 interviews he discovered varieties of

sexual behavior of which he had no previous knowledge.

But perhaps the most extraordinary thing about Kinsey was not the amount of research he accomplished (more than 18,000 interviews) but the ease with which he persuaded people to disclose intimate details of their sexual lives. Only 6 people out of those 18,000 became visibly upset in the course of an interview. Kinsey had a simplicity, a directness about him; he once approached a male prostitute in a bar used by homosexuals—a fairly daunting contact to make—and said, "I am Dr. Kinsey from Indiana University and I am making a study of sex behavior. May I buy you a drink?"

The man not only accepted the drink and cooperated fully himself, but persuaded other male prostitutes to do likewise. Dr. Kinsey's scientific interests were in sexual intercourse; his own genius undoubtedly lay in social intercourse.

Significant Beginnings

His background could hardly have been expected to produce a revolutionary in the world of sexual research. He was born in 1894, to deeply religious middle-class parents in New Jersey; he was a delicate child, and in order to toughen him, his parents encouraged him to join the Boy Scouts, where he became one of

America's first Eagle Scouts. He made his first contribution to science during his scouting days, by publishing a paper called "What Do Birds Do When It Rains?" In the light of Kinsey's later publications, the title has great enchantment—and significance too, perhaps. To discover what birds do indeed do when it rains requires painstaking observation under difficult and uncomfortable circumstances. So was it with the later research.

Gall Wasps, then Sex

Kinsey progressed to Bowdoin College and received a B.Sc. in psychology when he was 22. He showed little interest in sex. "He was the young man who played the piano at fraternity dances while the others danced," said Dr. Wardell Pomeroy, one of his closest associates in later life. Another story of Kinsey's youth says a great deal about his background and upbringing; a fellow student and friend came to him and told him that he was deeply worried because he had been masturbating. Kinsey's solution was that they should kneel together and pray.

Having graduated, Kinsey became a Ph.D. in entomology (the study of insects) and dedicated himself to a study of gall wasps. These insects were his prime interest for the next 17 years—from 1920 to 1937. The gall wasps were even further removed from his ultimate study than the birds who did things in the rain—for the gall wasp is one of the comparatively few species which can reproduce without insemination of the female by the male. However, Kinsey displayed in their study the same painstaking care and devotion which characterized everything he did, and over a period of 20 years he collected about 4,000,000 of them. Pomeroy attributes to that study the development of Kinsey's genius for communication with people. He hiked around the country with a pack on his back in pursuit of his goal, sleeping out and introducing himself to the country people who told him where the most likely hunting grounds were. He learned to speak their language and to break down social barriers; he (and we who have benefited from his later research) owes his study of gall wasps a great deal.

He became a lecturer at Indiana University in 1920, where he met and married a chemistry student, Clara McMillan. They had four children and were extremely happy. Kinsey's path seemed set fair for a future with the wasps and his Clara and indeed until 1937 very little happened to interrupt this pattern. Then the university decided to inaugurate lectures on sex education and marriage and Kinsey was chosen to give them. One feels his suitability owed as much to his sexual respectability as his sexual knowledge.

So painstaking a researcher could hardly be expected to launch a course of lectures without a very thorough knowledge of his subject. A man who is still studying wasps after 17 years is clearly an information seeker of high caliber.

Kinsey set out to acquaint himself as closely with the subject of sexual behavior as he had with his wasps. Sexual research, and certainly sexual research of a statistical nature, was almost unknown—which was precisely why he undertook it. All the work done by people like Havelock Ellis, Freud or Krafft-Ebing was not, in Kinsey's view, entirely scientific.

He began by questioning 62 men and women who were associated in some way with his university. His method of gaining information was simple—he just asked. He believed passionately that the only satisfactory way to find things out was by personal interview, and he never changed his mind. But even at the peak of his investigations he never had more than eight interviewers on his staff at any one time—in fact six of them stayed with him throughout his entire career as a sexual researcher.

Discretion—and Ingenuity

Eighty-five percent of the 18,000 interviews were conducted either by Kinsey or Pomeroy. He was painstaking, patient—and inherently discreet. Every name, every piece of information was recorded in a code so secret that it was not even written down—it was taught verbally to the interviewers while they were being trained. Apart from the code's security benefits, it also enabled the interviewers to discuss their cases in public, without fear of giving offense. "So and so prefers Z to Cm," Pomeroy might remark to Kinsey—which would in fact mean so and so preferred having intercourse with animals rather than with his wife. A hard code to crack; Pomeroy did so once as a trainee, so another was immediately worked out. All the interviewees were volunteers. They were of every social group, every race, every creed—or every one that might reasonably be available to a researcher in the United States in the middle of the twentieth century.

Kinsey was also fanatical about his 100 percent sampling. Sampling is crucial in research. If you talk to 2 people from a group of 20, that is a meaningless sample from which to draw conclusions about that group. Kinsey would only be satisfied with the full 20.

One of his greatest triumphs in this direction came in a piece of deliciously neat table-turning; he was asked to lecture at a clinic, and was given the impression that his audience were interested and impressed with his research. On arrival, he found 30 almost overtly hostile psychiatrists, whose questioning at the end of the lecture was near-rude and hypercritical. Kinsey was short of data on psychiatrists at the time, and when the questioning was over, he informed the 30 learned gentlemen that he wanted their histories and in the cause of science he would expect them all to cooperate; they could scarcely refuse, and in fact none did.

Frigidity and Homosexuality

So what, then, through his 18,000 interviews, did he discover? One of his most remarkable findings was that hardly any women were frigid. Only about 2 percent were genuinely incapable of experiencing sexual arousal or orgasm. They were not necessarily going to enjoy it in sexual intercourse—in fact masturbation was a far more certain way of achieving it—but the equipment for enjoyment was there, just as it was in the male. What was more—and this gave rise to a lot of tight-lipped tut-tutting—Kinsey revealed that women who had enjoyed orgasm in premartial experience were far more likely to go on enjoying it after marriage—with obviously beneficial effects on the relationship.

Then there was homosexuality. Pre-Kinsey, you were either homosexual or you were not. Not so, said Kinsey. Lots of men carry on homosexual and heterosexual relationships at the same time. In fact he devised a homosexual rating scale, and asked men to rate their homosexual tendencies from six to zero—after they had given their histories. That was important. Because of what they had already revealed about themselves, the men were forced to give a more honest assessment. In fact, although only 4 percent of men were exclusively homosexual and never aroused by a woman, a full 37 percent had at least one homosexual experience between adolescence and old age. Revelations of this kind forced people

Keystone Press

to take a more tolerant view towards homosexuality. If nearly 40 percent of the men in any one group at any one time had had a homosexual experience, it was hard to demand that a convicted offender should be a social outcast.

Sexual Athletics

Perhaps the most startling findings of all were those about the sexual relations people were found to have with animals, chiefly household pets. One might well wonder how Kinsey persuaded people to part with such information. The key lay in the form the interview took. Each one was conducted in total privacy and the answers recorded in code. It would take on average from one-and-a-half to two hours and there was a systematic coverage of a basic number of about 350 items—which extended to a maximum of 521. A notable exception was a gentleman of 63, who claimed to have had sexual relations with 600 little boys, 200 little girls, countless adults and animals and many members of his own family. Getting his history took nearly 17 hours in all and, not surprisingly, formed the basis of almost an entire chapter in the "Male" volume.

Dr. Alfred Kinsey's findings have helped to bring about a better understanding of sexual behavior.

For the slightly more commonplace respondent, the art of interviewing lay in the pattern of questioning. He would be asked first about his birthplace, where he lived, his age and so on; his religious history, health, hobbies and interests. It was all very unthreatening. Then, having discussed his family background, he was asked about sex education. This would have taken place far enough in the past for him not to feel uneasy about talking. Gradually the interview would move forward into puberty, first sexual experiences, on into the recent past and then the present. By now the interviewee was so involved and interested in himself, so warmed by the natural, unemotional climate of the questioning, he would talk about anything. He often found it therapeutic. Dr. Kinsey got quite used to being told that his respondents felt that they should be paying him. The question which women found hardest to answer, incidentally, was not, as you might expect, about their extramarital affairs or homosexual relationships, but simply "How much

do you weigh?"

Another important facet of the Kinsey interviewing technique was to assume that every subject had engaged in every activity. The only question was *when*. This provided greater accuracy, because it was perfectly clear by the way the question was asked that the researcher would be surprised or shocked by nothing, so there was no reason to deny it.

The questioning was fast and furious, not just to enable Kinsey to reach his goal of 100,000 histories more quickly, but because the subject was more likely to answer honestly and spontaneously if he did not have much time to think.

A Storm of Controversy

The publication of Kinsey's findings caused an uproar; disgust was mixed with a hopeful disbelief. The books, not surprisingly, became best-sellers, more, perhaps, for their sensational content than their contribution to science. Libraries debated whether they should contain them; parents hastened to discourage their children from reading them. Kinsey's research funds were cut off by Dean Rusk, then president of the Rockefeller Foundation; one opponent declared his findings as revealing "a prevailing degradation in American morality" (for which he obviously, and most unfairly, blamed Kinsey personally); and a McCarthyite minister called the report "Communistic."

It was ironic that Kinsey's name should have become synonymous with sensationalism in sex, for he was simply a scientist, a researcher, who happened to have settled for a somewhat controversial study.

It might have been better for him to have stayed with his wasps; but it would have been the worse for us. For Kinsey's findings undoubtedly helped bring about a better understanding of sexual behavior. He was totally dispassionate in his work; he never judged or even evaluated sexual behavior. He set out to find out what people did, how they behaved, and then to report on those findings. After that, he had no further interest in the matter. It was up to others, the psychiatrists, the sociologists, to draw conclusions, to make further observation, to pontificate as they wished.

The sex therapists of today are fortunate to be working in so sympathetic a climate. That the climate has become more relaxed is undoubtedly due in very large part to Dr. Alfred Kinsey.

SEXUAL RESPONSE	ANGER
REDUCED SENSORY PERCEPTION	REDUCED SENSORY PERCEPTION
PUPIL DILATION	PUPIL DILATION
INVOLUNTARY VOCALIZATION	INVOLUNTARY VOCALIZATION
SALIVARY SECRETION	SALIVARY SECRETION
HYPERVENTILATION	HYPERVENTILATION
IRREGULAR BREATHING	IRREGULAR BREATHING
INCREASED BLOOD PRESSURE	INCREASED BLOOD PRESSURE
INCREASED PULSE RATE	(RARE) INCREASED PULSE RATE
INCREASED PERIPHERAL CIRCULATION	INCREASED PERIPHERAL CIRCULATION
REDUCED BLEEDING	REDUCED BLEEDING
INHIBITED GASTROINTERACTION	INHIBITED GASTROINTERACTION
ADRENALIN SECRETION	ADRENALIN SECRETION
RYTHMIC MUSCULAR MOVEMENT	
TUMESCENCE	
GENITAL SECRETION	
EJACULATION	
MUSCULAR TENSION	MUSCULAR TENSION
INCREASED MUSCULAR CAPACITY	INCREASED MUSCULAR CAPACITY
INVOLUNTARY MUSCULAR ACTIVITY	INCREASED MUSCULAR ACTIVITY

Ron Hayward

The sensationalism attached to the findings of Kinsey did much to obscure the fact that his close analysis of human sexual behavior went a long way towards answering some of the questions that had been puzzling the medical profession. One such question was the relationship between anger and sex. It had long been noted that bodily responses in anger and during sexual arousal were in many aspects similar. Freudian analysts in particular argued that anger—both concealed and expressed—was often the result of repressed sexuality. Kinsey showed that there certainly was a close parallel between sexual response and the physiology of anger. This table illustrates how sexual arousal can only be differentiated from anger by four bodily functions—rhythmic muscular movement, tumescence or swelling, genital secretion, and ejaculation. From this evidence, Kinsey hypothesized that if certain physiological elements were prevented from developing, the individual might be left in a state of anger. The fact that frustrated sexual responses so readily turn into anger might thus be explained. As Kinsey pointed out, in the lower mammals and in man anger and fighting easily turn into sexual response. Could this be the clue to love-hate relationships?

All you want to know about...

STRESS

Zip Art

Q DO YOU INHERIT A TENDENCY TO SUFFER FROM STRESS?

A Yes, unfortunately you do. The precise factors in a person's make-up, whether physiological or psychological, which make him susceptible to anxiety or conflict are not clearly understood but many scientists believe that they are genetically determined. For example, there is clear evidence that some of the major psychoses run in families in the same way as do tendencies towards particular physical diseases. On the other hand a condition of chronic stress is not merely dependent upon the individual's make-up but also upon the forces which operate in his working and domestic life. Thus even a person who comes from a family with a long history of stress may lead a relatively peaceful life if he lives in an environment which does not provoke conflict situations. One might add here that one should never lose sight of the fact that stress in the short term is a natural and healthy response. Anyone who was unfortunate enough to be born without the capacity to react in a "stressful" way would not last long in our essentially dangerous world.

CAN YOU SUFFER FROM STRESS AND NOT KNOW IT?

Yes you can, and what is more this is often the most damaging and upsetting manifestation of the problem. Not all the forces which threaten the individual and throw him into a state of physiological or psychological alert are immediately recognizable to him nor, even if they are recognized as threats, may they be easily identified or described in words. For example, a husband and wife may apparently have a normal and "satisfactory" marital relationship and yet major conflicts may arise which relate to unconscious likes or dislikes, conditioned by some neurotic behavior pattern or by attitudes carried over from the past. A wife may devote an abnormal amount of time to house cleaning, which could be her way of submerging basic anxieties about her husband's fidelity. The husband in turn may spend little of his spare time at home, because his psychological immaturity makes him wish to deny and reject the marriage to which he is socially committed. Here both sides may have unconscious goals—the wife's to retain her husband's love, the husband's to escape from what he believes to be a trap. There may be children involved to complicate the issue. As the goals are unconscious— and might even be denied by both parties if they were questioned about them—a state of chronic stress will exist. In this case the stress would be largely psychological and the bodily "state of alertness" would be maintained at a low level, but over a long period of time. Psychologists believe that it is from these unconscious stress situations that most major neurotic behavior patterns stem. The woman may devote all her energies and channel her stress into a compulsive concern with house cleanliness. The husband may expend his psychic energy on heavy social drinking, gambling, or other essentially wasteful activities. From these points, unless the stress-inducing conflict is somehow solved, the neuroses may escalate so that the wife becomes severely obsessive or depressed while the husband may push his social drinking into alcoholism, or his betting sprees into compulsive gambling. These are simply manufactured examples, but they indicate one classic point in understanding stress: body and mind should act in harmony and disruptive stimuli, when they occur, should induce corrective action. When the corrective action cannot be made or turns out to be inadequate, tension remains and will seek out a channel for escape. Stress problems are at their worst when the sufferer cannot identify their origins.

IS STRESS CONTAGIOUS?

Not in the strict sense of the word of course. Stress is a condition or state of the body and not a disease or substance of any kind. Nevertheless in a curious way a person under stress, either in the acute (short-term) or chronic (long-term) sense, can convey this feeling to others close to him. An example of the acute transfer of stress is when an individual, by revealing his own uncertainty or fear, may consciously or unconsciously signal this to others so that a panic ensues. Often an orderly crowd moving purposefully away from a dangerous situation, such as a fire, can be turned into a mindless rabble because an individual member of the group has signaled his own stress too strongly. Chronic stress may be equally inclined to spread. Symptoms of anxiety and general unhappiness which are a common result of stress can affect an entire family when only one member of it is really under stress. The same applies, on a lesser scale, to working groups in businesses, factories and even military units, where morale may be greatly affected if too many members of the group are suffering from chronic stress.

HOW CAN YOU PREVENT STRESS?

If you are going to live a real life in a real world, the answer is that you cannot hope to eliminate stress totally. The only alternative would be to lead a vegetablelike existence in which you never put yourself in any kind of threatening or conflict situation. Under such circumstances life might be safe—but very dull. Even then the penalties would be considerable; your muscles would atrophy through lack of use and you would get obese through lack of exercise. The best one can hope is not to attempt to avoid stressful situations altogether, but rather to do everything that one can to find solutions to them when they arise and avoid getting oneself into chronic conditions which produce unpleasant physical and psychological side effects. This may not be as difficult as it sounds. Often it is a matter merely of identifying the stressful situation—it is amazing how many people cannot see the wood for the trees in these circumstances. Here the role of the doctor or psychologist is obvious, though even a trusted friend can sometimes help in pointing out the origin of the conflict that is putting one under prolonged stress.

HOW DOES STRESS AFFECT SLEEP?

Sleep appears to be an automatic habit, so natural and universal that it is unnecessary for us to *strive* to achieve it. In point of fact complex physiological, neurological and biochemical changes occur in the body as the system switches from the waking to the sleeping state. Preparation for sleep is dependent upon a number of factors, and if these are not met sleep is stubborn to come. Apart from such obvious factors as achieving a comfortable place to rest, and making sure that there are coverings of some kind to prevent heat loss from the body, it is also essential to produce a relaxed frame of mind. Such a frame of mind is hard to define, but there will be few people who do not know what is meant by the expression. Most people, even if they suffer from stress only occasionally, will have noticed that a racing, hyperactive state of mind markedly inhibits the onset of sleep—a child, filled with excitement because it is Christmas Eve; a teenager concerned about an important social occasion on the next day; an adult who must face an important interview, etc. In these states the mind rehearses future events, setting up "goals," considering strategies which might help to achieve them, and testing and rejecting them in the fantasy world of the mind. When suitable solutions, or "pleasant fantasies," are circulating, sleep will often engulf the individual without warning. When the problem is a big one, and none of the tactics seem adequate to cope with it, the mind remains in a state of stress, and will continue to do so until some reasonable or satisfactory solutions are achieved. All people suffer periodically from this irritating phenomenon, but it should be clear that sleeplessness of this kind will be greatly increased when the problems, unmet goals, unsolved or ill-defined conflicts are many. Therefore the classic conditions of stress—the inability of the individual to meet his psychological and/or physiological goals—arise, and prolonged or chronic sleeplessness can result. The unfortunate consequences of this are that the sleeplessness itself in the long run makes the individual less efficient, less well-motivated and even less capable of coping with the challenges of life, and thus the problem is compounded. It is here that hypnotics, and sleeping pills of one kind or another, when prescribed in moderation by a doctor, can be of enormous benefit. More satisfactory still is a period of vacation, and total withdrawal from the provocative conditions which have been causing stress to build up.

IS STRESS AFFECTED BY THE TYPE OF FOOD WE EAT?

Not really, if we discount drugs or foods containing special stimulants acting directly upon the central nervous system to provoke excitable and ultimately stressful behavior. Of course, technically speaking, alcohol is a food and while it initially acts as a central nervous system *depressant* and therefore reduces stress symptoms, its prolonged use can affect sleep patterns, reduce the overall efficiency of brain and muscular coordinating system and ultimately aggravate long-term stress conditions. But when most people ask this question, they are thinking of foods of the breakfast-lunch-and-dinner varieties. Here the evidence is that there is no specific food which induces stress. On the other hand many people who are at risk are advised by their physicians to avoid cholesterol-rich diets. The reason for this is obvious enough, for, as we have said, general physical and mental excitement saturates the system with fatty acids and if these are already present in large quantities then their effects are multiplied. For anyone living a high-stress life, therefore, certain foods should definitely be avoided, but this is not to say that these foods actually produce stress on their own.

DOES STRESS AFFECT YOUR SEX LIFE?

Yes, it can affect it in a number of ways. When people are afflicted by anxieties due to stress, a normal sex life is often one of the first casualties. When under stress the individual's mental energy may be diverted into a constant search for solutions to the multitude of problems, great or small, in which he has become enmeshed. Little of this effort remains to feed the powerhouse of the sex drive. An uneasy mind also tends to inhibit sexual performance, and impotence in men and frigidity in women may be a consequence. Sometimes however there is a curious inversion of this rule. People with one or more of the major psychological conflicts inducing a prolonged state of stress may attempt to deny to themselves the existence of the conflicts and thus divert surplus psychic energy into alternative channels. This can lead to an abnormal involvement with sex which can cause disruption of one's domestic life (because one or other of the partners, dissatisfied with the marital relationship, embarks on a series of "affairs") or even of one's working life which can occasionally be subjugated to an overwhelming concern with sex. It also means that the conflicts, because they are "denied," remain unresolved.

WHAT ARE THE PHYSIOLOGICAL EFFECTS OF STRESS?

Remember that when we speak of stress we are referring to the state of body and mind which follows the onset of a threatening stimulus and persists until the stimulus or the threatening circumstances are removed or dealt with in some way. The first thing to consider therefore is what changes take place in the body when a stressful situation occurs. These vary with intensity and depend upon circumstances but in general they are as follows. Firstly, salivation is restrained (which is why you find it so difficult to speak when you are "nervous"), secondly movements of the stomach and intestine are inhibited (hence the "sinking feeling") and digestion inter-

rupted. Excessive interference with gastric operation of this kind is presumed to lie behind ulcer conditions or nervous stomachs. Colon and bladder activities are also restricted, which may account for the chronic constipation which affects many stressfully anxious individuals. Heartbeat is raised and blood is taken away from the skin and concentrated in muscles and brain, which, incidentally, is the reason why people go pale with fright. Speeding up heart rate and constricting blood vessels also make the blood pressure rise. These gross physiological changes are accompanied by hormonal effects which are also part

of the alerting response. The most significant of these is the release of adrenaline, which induces the increased heart rate but, more significantly from the long-term point of view, causes the liver to pump sugar into the bloodstream to meet the expected increase in energy requirements posed by the emergency. There is also a massive outpouring of cholesterol, an important fatty acid which supplies energy. In normal circumstances, once the "emergency" is dealt with the body returns to normal and the extra sugar, cholesterol, etc., if not used up, will gradually dissipate. In the individual under constant stress, however, the system rarely returns to normal and in due course the high blood sugar and cholesterol levels, to say nothing of the extra strain on the heart and other organs, begin to have harmful effects.

WHAT IS THE MOST STRESSFUL THING THAT YOU CAN DO?

This depends enormously upon the individual. What is stressful for one person may not necessarily be so for another and in the long run it is a matter of how well one is able to control the pressures and challenges that life presents. Most people gradually learn what their own limitations are and manage to avoid exceedingly

stressful situations. Others seem to thrive on stress, though what they actually thrive on is the solving of problems which to other people would appear stressful. There are however a number of universally stress-producing situations and almost the most important of these is one of the most common activities that modern man indulges in—driving an automobile. This is a classic stress-producing situation. When driving, people are bottled up in their motor cars, anxious to get somewhere and yet constantly frustrated by overcrowded roads and the belligerency of other drivers. Major changes in the body's physiology and biochemistry take place as the result of the challenges and frustrations. In particular, cholesterol is pumped out in great quantities, but instead of being used up in the bursts of physical energy which the stressful situation demands, it remains suspended in the blood as the driver sits impotently behind the wheel. Samples of blood taken from racing motorists show it to have a milky consistency due to the colossal quantities of fatty acids suspended in it. Commuter drivers who spend hours of every day in traffic jams are even worse off and the fatty acids eventually cling to the arterial walls. In the long term, regular commuting may put the driver more at risk of death from a heart attack (though not necessarily at the wheel) than from an automobile accident itself.

WHAT IS THE EFFECT OF NOISE ON STRESS?

Contrary to popular belief, noise in itself does not induce stress. This may seem an unlikely statement to people living near a busy highway or under the flight path of a big airport. However experimental evidence accumulated over many decades has shown that noise on its own is not a stress-inducing stimulus. What does affect human behavior and inhibit performance both in psychological and physiological tasks is variation of noise. The distinction is not as subtle as it seems. Variation in the level and type of noise represents constantly changing input to the nervous system, which in turn produces persistent distraction for the individual from the task he is performing. Whether the task is cooking, reading, talking, trying to go to sleep or whatever, the persistent shifts of attention which bursts of noise provoke prevent the individual's mental and physical goals from being achieved. Stress inevitably follows.

Visual perception

Depth Perception

Close one eye. With one finger, try to touch the edge of your chair arm or a nearby table, just grazing the edge. Try it again with an object two to two-and-a-half feet in front of you. Did you manage the first time, or did you go too far in either direction? Most people misjudge the distance for the first few trials, because we use information from *both* eyes to perceive depth. The fields of vision of our two eyes overlap, giving an impression of depth and solidity. Because our eyes are separated in our heads, the left eye does not get exactly the same view as the right, and the images are combined in the brain.

Stereoscopic Pictures

With the use of a mirror or prism, it is possible to give flat pictures an artificial third dimension; this works on the same principle as the stereoscope, which was at one time introduced into movies. In the stereo-scopic photographs below, the left-hand pictures are not simply reverse images of the right; they are taken from slightly different points of view. Place a pocket mirror against the right side of your nose, with your eyes about six inches above the pictures of Stonehenge. Your right eye should be looking at the *reflection* of the right-hand picture and your left eye directly at the left-hand picture. Adjust the mirror until the images coincide, and you will see the stones become "solid." Try it with the second pair of pictures. The slight difference in view-point gives the impression of depth.

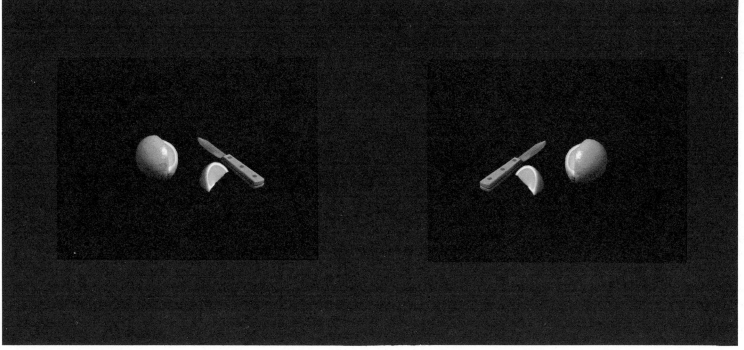

Bob Estall

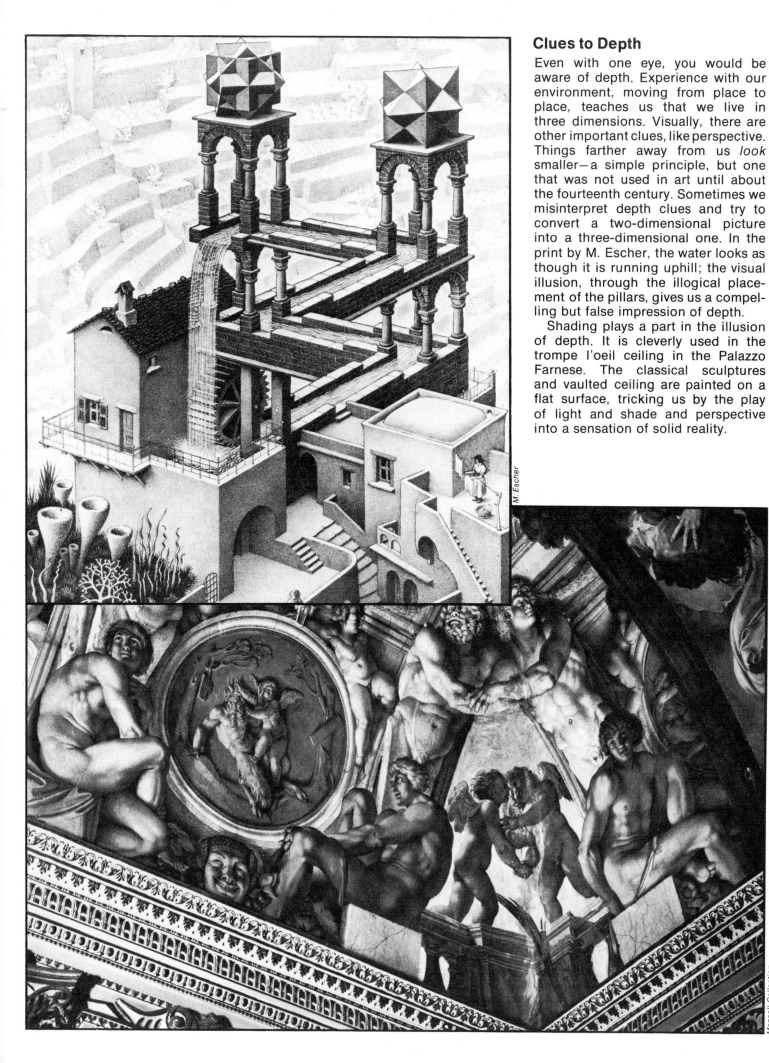

Clues to Depth

Even with one eye, you would be aware of depth. Experience with our environment, moving from place to place, teaches us that we live in three dimensions. Visually, there are other important clues, like perspective. Things farther away from us *look* smaller—a simple principle, but one that was not used in art until about the fourteenth century. Sometimes we misinterpret depth clues and try to convert a two-dimensional picture into a three-dimensional one. In the print by M. Escher, the water looks as though it is running uphill; the visual illusion, through the illogical placement of the pillars, gives us a compelling but false impression of depth.

Shading plays a part in the illusion of depth. It is cleverly used in the trompe l'oeil ceiling in the Palazzo Farnese. The classical sculptures and vaulted ceiling are painted on a flat surface, tricking us by the play of light and shade and perspective into a sensation of solid reality.

M. Escher

Mansell Collection

Kim Sayer

The cleverer sex?

The battle of the sexes has been raging for centuries, and it seems to be a stand-off. In dealing with each other at least, men and women seem to give as good as they get. But can we say that one is actually more intelligent than the other?

In the days before the suffragette movement and Women's Lib it used to be taken for granted that men were intellectually superior to women; laws were framed to protect women against their assumed foolishness, putting a male (father, husband, brother) in charge of their affairs at all times. The apparent absence of female genius in any important sphere—science, sculpture, mathematics, drama, painting, politics (with the possible exception of novel writing)—seemed to support this argument.

Remnants of this attitude linger on; we still say that women successful in business or in academic careers or in medicine have a "masculine mind." Objective facts were hard to come by

until the turn of the century, and alternative theories, such as the fairly obvious one that women were culturally and socially so handicapped that whatever intelligence they had was prevented from manifesting itself, were seldom considered.

The development of intelligence tests changed the position drastically, and we now have certain clear-cut evidence to show that these views are quite wrong. From the very first, girls and women were found to be equal to boys and men on any of the most widely used intelligence tests; when slight differences were found, usually among younger children, girls if anything were superior to boys.

To some extent this exact equality

may be an artefact; the makers of intelligence tests, finding that on the whole there were few differences between the sexes, tended to avoid items which did show such differences; if they did not omit such items, they tended to balance an item favoring the males by another item favoring the females. Such equalization could not have happened had not the sexes been approximately equal in any case, but the equality in IQ between the sexes hides two important differences which may have far-reaching consequences for society in general.

The first major difference between men and women relates to the spread of intelligence. This is not equal; there are more very bright men, just as there are more very dull men. There are more women with average IQs, shading into the bright and dull regions of intelligence.

It has been suggested that this difference in distribution of IQ may be responsible for the remarkable fact that men are greatly overrepresented both among the mentally defective and among the geniuses. The argument is an attractive one. If there are more men with very low IQs, and if very low IQs are closely identified with mental defect, then an explanation of the predominance of men in the mentally defective category seems obvious. Similarly, genius requires high IQ; there are more men with high IQs, and consequently we may have here an easy explanation of the otherwise rather puzzling predominance of men among the outstanding persons of every age. But inviting as these speculations may be, there are reasons for distrusting such an obvious and convenient explanation.

The Making of a Genius

The act of certification of a person as mentally defective is a social act which takes into account many factors quite independent of IQ; indeed, intelligence testing in institutions for mental defectives has unearthed individuals with quite high IQs—the highest to date was 125! Youngsters with psychopathic personalities are sometimes sent to such institutions for want of a better place to send them to, and they are often of average or even superior intelligence—and nearly always male! Furthermore, men are required in our society to earn a living; a low IQ may make this extremely difficult, and thus finally result in their being certified.

Women are not equally likely to be required to earn a living; they may live at home until married, and after marriage their low IQ may impose a burden on their husbands, without leading to certification. There are thus all sorts of purely social and administrative reasons which may account for the observed excess of males among the mentally defective.

The same is true of genius. While there are thousands of people with high IQs there are very few geniuses. Without a doubt, there are enough women with very high IQs to provide a quota of geniuses; the reason for their failure to do so must be found elsewhere.

One cause often presented lies in the greater aggressiveness, dominance, assertiveness and sheer bullheadedness of men—all qualities

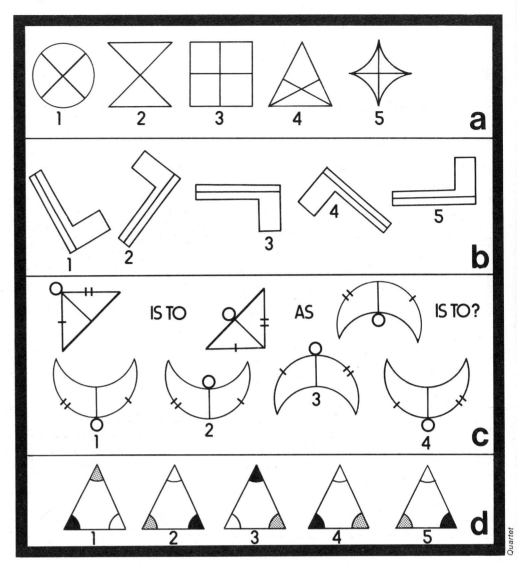

often connected with the budding genius, and possibly necessary to carry him to success. These personality qualities are closely linked with male hormones, and may therefore not be accidentally associated with the male. However, there is no evidence to show that any geniuses, past or present, have had a greater amount of male hormone than average, or that females who have achieved eminence in a field possess as much of this hormone as eminent males in the field or indeed more than ordinary females have either.

Sex-linked Abilities

Another cause might be the obvious social disability which still makes it much more difficult for women, particularly women who wish to marry and have children, to compete successfully with men. Men can devote themselves more single-mindedly to the pursuit of a career than can women. In certain countries that have shaken off traditional male-female roles, the Soviet Union for example, women actually predominate in fields like medicine.

Tests of this sort assess your visual perception and ability to manipulate shapes in space. For problems a, b and d, find the odd one out; for problem c, select which pattern completes the relationship. According to psychologists, the dice are loaded against women!

Another major difference between men and women relates to the pattern of abilities which go to make up their respective IQs. Alfred Binet, who designed the first practically used IQ test, was insistent that problems as varied as possible should be included in this test; he used different abilities (verbal, numerical, spatial), as well as different mental mechanisms (reasoning, memory, suggestion, etc.). The IQ in a sense is the average of all these different types of mental abilities, applied to all sorts of different mental materials. Even though two people may achieve the same total IQ score, one may have better verbal ability, another better numerical ability. One may have an outstanding reasoning ability, and the other might

Typical tests on which girls are superior is the so-called synonyms/antonyms test. In this, the person tested indicates which of the two words printed on each line mean the same as, or in some cases the opposite of, the first word.

a. NONCHALANT   melancholy   zealous
b. QUANDARY   dilemma   quadrant
c. DECREE   ordinance   edict
d. DIABOLICAL   ridiculous   angelic
e. CHAGRIN   vexation   sneer
f. OBDURATE   intractable   vigilant
g. SANG FROID   composure   climax
h. INTREPID   silent   timorous

Women are superior to men with respect to the executive aspects of language but this superiority does not apply to verbal reasoning, i.e. to reasoning in which the problem is stated in words, and where the process of reasoning is most likely carried out verbally. On a test like the following, women would not have an advantage over men, the results for both groups being about equal. Here the testee is required to formulate the relation that is implied between the first two words, then choose from the five alternatives in brackets the one which when paired with the third word extends this relationship.

For example:
CLOCK—TIME: SCALES—(FISH, SCALP, BEAM, WEIGHT, BALANCE)

Here the first word in each pair is a device for measuring an abstract quality, signified by the second word.
a. HAUGHTY—PRIDE: QUIVERING—(QUAKE, FOOL, SHIVERING, FEAR, SHAKING)
b. WARRANT—ARREST: LICENSE—(SWIM, DOG, AUTOMOBILE, CERTIFICATE, WED)
c. CHAPEL—CATHEDRAL: WARD—(ROOM, INSANE, HOSPITAL, HOARD, PATIENT)
d. INNOCENCE—ACQUITTAL: GUILT—(ERROR, CRIME, POLICE, GUILD, CONVICTION)
e. MUSCLE—CONTRACTION: NERVE—(EXPANSION, SERVE, FIBER, MONKEY, CONDUCTION)
f. MANNERS—GENTLEMAN: SYMPTOM—(DISEASE, DOCTOR, SIMPLE, POVERTY, SIGN)
g. PENSION—VETERAN: INSURANCE—(POLICY, AGENT, COMPENSATION, ASSURANCE, BENEFICIARY)
h. IRON—MAGNET: MOTH—(DUST, MYTH, FUR, INSECT, LIGHT)

have an excellent memory.

Thus the possibility arises that men and women, although equal in total score, are yet different with respect to certain strengths and weaknesses. Men might be better with respect to one type of ability, women with respect to another. This indeed seems to be the case, and the particular pattern of abilities, as related to sex, has received much attention from psychologists in recent years.

We may begin with very elementary abilities which are not very highly correlated with IQ. Women have lower touch and pain thresholds than men; this greater sensitivity to touch and pain has been observed from birth, and is characteristic of the female sex. Women also have better auditory discrimination; men, on the other hand, are better at visual discrimination. These differences, too, are found very early in life; when only a few weeks old, girls show more interest in tonal patterns, while boys are more concerned with visual stimuli. Studies of sexual stimulation bear out this differentiation—men are more responsive than women to visual erotic stimuli, as any pornographer will testify. Women are more dependent on tactile stimulation. These differences, as well as the related one of greater female susceptibility and sensitivity to olfactory stimuli (odors), seem connected to the presence of sex hormones. In other words these are not the accidental results of social conditioning, but are genetically linked with the sex of the individual.

When we turn to more complex abilities, we find that men excel in spatial ability, that is, in the visuo-spatial skills required to organize and relate visual stimuli to their spatial contexts, and to manipulate visual material imaginatively.

Natural Talkers
Spatial ability is better developed in males in other species than the human too; in rats and chimpanzees we find the same superiority, and we now think that there is a genetic link between a person's sex and his visuo-spatial ability. If social customs and habits exert an influence, it cannot be very large or decisive.

If females are inferior in respect to visuo-spatial ability, they come into their own with respect to verbal skills. Girls learn to talk more easily than boys; they have a better vocabulary than boys of comparable age, and they articulate better. Altogether, they are superior with respect to all aspects of language usage. Writing, spelling,

grammar and sentence construction all show girls ahead of boys. Furthermore, their particular ability at even quite early ages predicts well their final IQs when they reach adolescence or adulthood—this is not so with boys, who develop more erratically.

Memory and Understanding
Another ability in which women excel is rote memory. They are able to hold in their memory store various unrelated and personally irrelevant facts, for short periods of time, where men tend to remember only coherent and/or personally relevant material. In school work, girls traditionally have learned by committing material to memory, while boys have tended to try to master the underlying principles. It is not known whether this difference is really sex-linked, or whether it is due to differences in upbringing, social expectations, and the like.

But without any biological evidence to the contrary it seems quite likely due to the fact that a girl's role has been to conform to standards and to please by supplying what is demanded: straying too far from fashion will not attract the best mate. A man on the other hand has been expected to shape events to his own needs and to provide the organizing force from within himself.

Mechanically Minded
In the same vein, although boys and men tend to do better on tests of numerical and mathematical abilities, this is not necessarily so when dealing with problems of purely "mechanical" arithmetic. It is when more complex mathematical reasoning and the manipulation of abstract numerical entities are called for that this superiority becomes apparent.

Men tend to be better than women at mechanical tasks, probably because of their proficiency in visuo-spatial abilities. This superiority is particularly marked when a task calls for the comprehension of mechanical relationships; as far as manual dexterity is concerned women tend to perform better. These differences may be responsible for the sorts of careers into which men and women tend to drift: men predominate in technical, constructive and motor repair jobs, while women predominate in secretarial jobs, and assembly jobs requiring deft use of their hands.

Although it would not be reasonable to forget the biologically determined abilities which make such differentiation meaningful, the underlying forces again might well be social. Manual dexterity depends as much on a frame of mind, a willingness to do, say, assembly-line work because it is the only employment available, as it does on nimble fingers.

Still, it is interesting to note that the basic dissimilarity between the sexes, visuo-spatial versus linguistic skills, may be related to a similar cerebral difference. The right hemisphere is more concerned with perceptual, motor, spatial and quite generally non-linguistic skills; the left hemisphere, on the other hand, is concerned almost entirely with language. (This is true of most right-handed people.) There is some evidence that in young children growth of the nerve formations in various areas of the brain is more advanced in the left hemi-

Psychological tests show that women have better memories than men. "Mastermind," a prestigious British television quiz show, has been won consistently by women, two of whom are pictured here. Possibly their coolness under pressure was the key factor.

sphere in girls, and in the right hemisphere in boys. This may be the key in the biological basis for the differences in ability between the sexes; or it could simply mean that relative growth in these areas is the result of increased usage of certain faculties due to differences in early conditioning and external stimuli.

What *is* Intelligence?

Which is the cleverer sex? The emotional nature of this issue often clouds and distorts the few facts there are, and to complicate matters further, we are not even very sure what the question involves.

Intelligence is usually described as "the ability to adapt." It is, at best, a nebulous concept, and one not susceptible to easy measurement. Makers of intelligence tests have tended to define it by the factors they can best measure, like verbal or visuo-spatial abilities. But there are, we know, other qualities often associated with proficiency in given situations that have so far been much more difficult to quantify and reduce to statistics: traits like creativity, common sense and intuition. And how far any of the qualities contributing to intelligence are influenced by persistence, optimism or other social factors, quite apart from a person's biological maleness or femaleness, we still cannot really tell.

Answers to sample questions

Visuo-spatial ability

a. 4. (All the other drawings can be turned upside down without making any difference.)

b. 3. (All the other figures can be rotated into each other.)

c. 1. (The main figure is turned over, and the little circle is transferred to the other side.)

d. 4. (The black, white and shaded portions rotate positions counterclockwise; in 4 the shaded and white portions are in the wrong positions.)

Synonyms/antonyms

a. Zealous	e. Vexation
b. Dilemma	f. Intractable
c. Edict	g. Composure
d. Angelic	h. Timorous

Correlation

a. Fear	e. Conduction
b. Wed	f. Disease
c. Hospital	g. Beneficiary
d. Conviction	h. Light

Choosing partners

What is it that makes us fall in love with a particular person and then want to marry them? Does like attract like or is the attraction of opposites more usual? Is it possible to tell the difference between romantic love and an intense liking for someone?

Most of us, at some time in our lives, experience the emotional upheaval best described as romantic love. It is universally agreed to be one of the most mysterious, intense and personal experiences that ever befalls us. What makes humans, with such dizzying frequency, fall in love? It is certainly not a rational process, yet Cupid's arrow does not strike entirely haphazardly either: the underlying emotional factors are as strong and inescapable as passion itself.

An attempt to make a distinction between romantic love and intense liking was once made by the Harvard psychologist Zick Rubin. Through the use of attitude tests he found that men associated love and liking more strongly than women—which supports the popular notion that women discriminate more sharply between the two sentiments. Women are apparently more likely to fall in love with somebody they do not like (in the sense they would not choose them as

a same-sex friend).

The "love scores" of men (for their women) and women (for their men) were almost identical, suggesting that the two sexes love to a similar degree. However, the women tended to *like* their men more than their men liked them—especially as indicated by ratings on attributes such as intelligence, good judgement and leadership potential—and to *love* their same-sex friends more than men did.

Psychoanalysts have observed that

Mick Brownfield

Pushing a button may seem a facetious way to choose a mate. But the dictates of the subconscious can be just as automatic, if slightly more subtle. Still, a marriage partner usually fulfills some basic psychological need, whether the lovers know it or not.

the process of falling in love appears to involve a kind of regression to childlike behavior. The forms of intimacy indulged in by lovers are certainly reminiscent of parent-child contact—hand-holding, embracing, kissing and baby-talk.

Sex and Affection

This analogy between parental care and the behavior of lovers is intuitively appealing. It suggests that romantic love is derived from our parental "instincts" and our need for security and protection dating from birth. However, the Freudians try to have it both ways, for at other times they argue that, in fondling their children, parents are unconsciously lavishing sexual behavior on them (i.e. that parental care is derived from adult sex drive). It is difficult to see how we can choose between these two opposite theories, but it seems probable that the romantic love experience involves the satisfaction (and sometimes frustration) of *both* our primary needs, sex and affection, which would help to explain the striking intensity of the emotions involved in love.

The ethologists from Lorenz to Morris have also noted that the origins

of love may be traced to parent-child intimacy. Whereas other animals separate completely from their parents to participate in an open power struggle, man is expected to love and respect his parents throughout life. Thus human love is seen as based upon an "infantile passion" that is not applicable to other species.

Another idea put up by the ethologists is that the evolution of a long term bond (love) between man and woman was necessary because of the long period for which their offspring are dependent upon them. Whereas for most animals copulation serves only a reproductive function, human evolution has also permitted sexual behavior to serve the purpose of maintaining the bond between a couple.

Who Will You Marry?

But, even more perplexing considering the number of astounding and ostensibly unsuitable matches we have all seen, what determines *who* you will fall in love with? Or *who* your future marriage partner will be? There are two current theories about this and they seem to be quite opposed, though both views have some validity.

One theory is that we fall in love with people who are *similar* to our-

selves ("like marries like"), while the other is that we choose a partner who *complements* us in some way ("opposites attract").

To begin with, a couple have to meet before they can fall in love and people of similar social class, race and religion tend to live in the same neighborhood. Obviously, we also tend to choose somebody of a similar age to ourselves, although on average the male is about two years older than the woman.

"Likes" v. "Opposites"

It is popularly believed that this age differential results from women maturing earlier, but it is more likely to happen because a woman's attractiveness is more physically based than a man's (his being based to a greater extent on status and achievement). Thus the desirability of a man continues to increase for some time beyond the teenage years, while that of a woman may perhaps decline.

Physical attractiveness is another area where the similarity theory of partner choice seems to apply. In an ingenious study, an American psychologist obtained a selection of wedding photographs and cut them apart so as to separate the married couples. The individual portraits were rated by a group of people who did not know how they had been originally paired off and therefore were unable to tell how another had viewed them. Their ratings revealed a very high correlation between the attractiveness of the person in the portrait and the observer's own attractiveness. The association was not perfect because there are many other factors than looks that affect each individual's eligibility.

The "opposites attract" theory has its most obvious support in connection with sex in the sense of gender. In general, we fall in love with a member of the opposite sex—the exceptional couples being regarded as deviant, although our tolerance of them has increased markedly in recent years. There are also a number of temperamental and personality characteristics for which a complementary approach appears to be appropriate. For example, a person who is dominant in social situations and likes to

Till Death Us Do Part

Divorce seems to have become almost fashionable in the twentieth century. Nearly everyone falls in love at one time or another, but the number of couples who actually stay together decreases every year.

This is especially so in Western countries like the United States and Britain. For example, in 1961 some 25,394 British marriages ended in divorce. Ten years later this figure had nearly tripled to 74,437.

The marriages of the famous which last are much in the public eye. What brought them together and how have they kept their love alive?

For example, the Duke of Windsor gave up a throne to marry Mrs. Wallace Warfield Simpson, the woman he loved. She was American, a divorcee, and a commoner, hardly the sort of person the public expected a member of the British royal family to marry. But they stayed together until his death.

When Richard Burton and Elizabeth Taylor married no one expected the match to last more than a few years. She had been billed on the screen as a sex symbol and he was a serious actor. Although they often came close to breaking up—and, in fact, have now done so—their marriage was still a long one.

Another actress who was a sex symbol, Sophia Loren, astonished millions by marrying a man much older than herself. Producer Carlo Ponti was not the kind of husband most people would have expected the Italian starlet to choose. But they too have had a long-lasting marriage.

Research has shown that love can be a basically selfish emotion. You want someone because you believe they are good for you or you are good for them. You may love someone because they excite your imagination. Or the person you love may attract you because they can help you to get ahead socially. Some people love another person who grants them sympathy and approval. Famous or anonymous, a complex variety of motives lead people into love relationships.

But staying in love is quite another matter. Every couple experiences their rapture in the beginning as a deep and caring relationship. Often though the magic dies and the marriage goes on the rocks. To keep your love match fresh you will have to use your imagination. Love is a lifelong lesson.

Ponti/Loren

Popperfoto

Taylor/Burton

The Duke and Duchess of Windsor

Popperfoto

do a lot of talking might find himself drawn towards a quiet, submissive partner. But this is actually a general law of personal relationships; we are usually attracted to people who appear to have something to offer to us.

According to the categories of P. H. Wright, a person may have *stimulation value* (e.g. be interesting, imaginative and introduce you to new ideas and activities), *utility value* (e.g. be helpful, rich, drive a car), or *ego-support value* (e.g. provide sympathy, encouragement and approval). All of these "economic" factors appear to operate in choosing a lover just as much as any other kind of friend.

Another important factor is approval. E. Aronson and D. Linder found that we are obviously unlikely to favor people who persist in making uniformly derogatory comments about us. But while we like people who are always complimentary about us, we tend to prefer those whose comments about us progress from unfavorable to favorable. It would seem that the best way to win new friends (and lovers) is to start by appearing to dislike them (without being too insulting), then show progressive interest and approval.

Parental Substitutes

The Freudians believe that in choosing a marriage partner we may be seeking a substitute for the opposite-sex parent as a means of resolving the so-called Oedipus complex. There is no real evidence to support this theory, although a study conducted by Alan Miller of the University of California, Los Angeles, is interesting in connection with it.

Miller had a group of women rank a series of photos of male physiques from those that looked "most like their father" to those that looked "least like their father"; later they were asked to choose a physique that they would most desire in a lover. There was a marked tendency for them to choose in a lover a physique that was either *most* or *least* like their perceived father. While not constituting proof of the Freudian position, this study does suggest that the nature of the bond to the opposite-sex parent may influence the choice of mate.

Perhaps the most interesting question of all and, oddly, the one that has

Marshall Cavendish

**Left: Sex appeal plays an undeniable part in winning a mate. It is harder to define than some of the other elements that bind two people together, but no one can ignore its magical force.
Right: "Putting on a face" is a more artificial way to attract a man. Here the *same* versatile woman styles herself to appeal to four different men. Her props and objectives: conservative cashmere (banker), hippie gear (bearded artist), trendy hat and make-up (male model), sophisticated hair style (mustachioed ad man). But insincere posing does not bode well for an honest relationship.**

Ron Embleton

been least researched, concerns the conditions which favor the development of romantic love. Here, in the absence of scientific evidence, we fall back on folklore and conjecture.

The Anatomy of Romance

We seem to have a tendency to fall in love following a *change of environment*, the classic example being holiday and shipboard romances. No doubt this is because we are, or feel ourselves to be, remote and released from family ties and other responsibilities, which would otherwise inhibit the development of the romantic experience. Alcohol, music, or unspoiled natural surroundings are also likely to facilitate the development of love in the same way.

Note that here romantic love is conceived as an antisocial force. Society is hypocritical with regard to love and often redefines the word for its own purposes. The dictum "sex is all right provided it goes with love" usually means "no sex unless you are, or intend to get, married." Moreover,

when romantic love threatens institutional marriage, society's preference becomes quite clear.

Another factor apparently favoring the emergence of love is *arousal*. It does not seem to matter whether the arousing experience is positive (e.g. excitement or success arising out of amateur dramatics or passing an examination) or basically unpleasant (e.g. danger, fear, pain), but ideally it should occur as a shared emotional experience. A classic experiment by S. Schachter showed that people who had been made anxious in an experimental situation developed a strong tendency towards affiliation with others in a similar plight.

A third idea which appears frequently in intuitive writings about love is that the presence of some *obstacle* in the path of the relationship—and especially something which hinders sexual fulfillment within it—is also likely to heighten the experience of mutual love. But unreciprocated love is more likely here to result eventually in a "sour grapes" type of reaction

Can you match up the couples? Outside observers are usually quite successful in this. Values and life styles (often indicated by appearance) tend to coincide, and mates are frequently on the same level of the "looks scale." Here, "likes" did attract: 1c, 2a, 3b.

("She does not appreciate me, therefore she must be a silly cow"). The mechanisms operating here are very complex, however, and probably not independent of the effects which have already been described.

The factors influencing the development of love provide an exciting field for future research, but we must await an adequate system for classifying the many different types of love—infatuation, sexual attraction, companionate married love, brotherly love, and so on—with precise definitions and behavior patterns appropriate to each category. For otherwise science will never be able to add anything to the insights of poets and philosophers into the mysteries of love.

All you want to know about...

STRESS STRESS STRESS STRESS STRESS STRESS

Faulkner Marks

Q **WHAT IS THE BEST KNOWN THEORY OF STRESS?**

A Theories of stress until quite recently were very tentative and ambiguous, probably because of a disagreement over the definition of stress itself. One of the few overall theories of stress, and perhaps the one most widely accepted at the present time, is that of Professor Hans Selye of the University of Montreal. He has introduced the concept of what he calls the general adaptation syndrome (G.A.S.), which defines the response of body and brain to stress agents. The pattern of stress itself follows three courses. First is *the alarm reaction*, the system's initial response to the stressors (which may be physiological or psychological). This is followed by *the stage of resistance*, when body and/or mind attempt to deal with the problems precipitated by the stressors. And finally there is *the stage of exhaustion*, at which the resistances prove inadequate and a mental breakdown or severe physical illness ensues. Throughout the day all human beings and animals find themselves involved in stage one of the G.A.S. and some degree of stage two inevitably follows. It is stage two that constitutes stress itself and it is the

amount of time which we remain in this stage that determines to a large degree our psychological and physiological well-being in life.

CAN ANIMALS SUFFER FROM STRESS?

Yes, in fact many of the most revealing studies of stress have been performed with experimental animals. The physiologist Pavlov, for example, trained a dog to salivate when it was shown a picture of a circle, by presenting it with food whenever a circle was shown. He also showed animals pictures of very flat ellipses, giving them electric shocks as he did so. After they had been thoroughly conditioned to associate food with a circle and pain with a flat ellipse, he gradually began to change the circle into an ellipse, and the ellipse into a circle. Initially the animals responded fairly confidently and appropriately, but as the "circle" and "ellipse" stimuli became more and more alike they began to show agitation, and in due course exhibited behavior of the "nervous breakdown" variety. Experimental animals subjected to weeks and months of such treatment began to develop physical symptoms such as persistent high blood pres-

sure, stomach ulcers and the like which are observed in many humans who suffer from long-term stress. In even more peculiar experiments performed recently in America, scientists trained monkeys to give each other electric shocks when certain stimuli were presented. Pairs of monkeys were employed, one of which had to sit and await the shock, while the other learned to give it at the appropriate signal from the experimenter. Both monkeys (not surprisingly) showed increasing signs of stress but with the creature actually delivering the shock suffering the most. These "executive" monkeys, as they were called, frequently developed stomach ulcers as the result of the stress they had been subjected to.

ARE SOME NATIONALITIES MORE LIKELY TO SUFFER FROM STRESS?

If you take a nation on average, the answer is probably yes. This is partly because of inherited characteristics which tend to be spread to some degree among national groups, but it may also be due to environmental and cultural factors. We have learned that stress will be more likely to occur in any person or group of people who live in an environment where their nervous systems are constantly challenged and frequently pushed to their limits. Thus nations with high economic, industrial and intellectual incentives will, as a group, be more likely to be at risk from stress than those with a simpler way of life and an agriculturally based, leisurely managed economy. Cultural factors are also important inasmuch as in some societies it is considered to be reasonable and normal to "show your emotions" (the "Latin temperament") and in others such behavior is considered to be improper (the British "stiff upper lip"). These behavior patterns are clearly culturally determined. Such external signals may give a misleading picture however and it could be that individuals inclined to uninhibited displays of emotions may end up being "less stressed" than those who prefer to present a cool exterior to their fellow men.

ARE THERE ANY TIPS TO HELP AVOID STRESS?

Stress is a condition of living, and as such cannot be totally avoided. Nevertheless there are ways in which you can provide some degree of psychic armor against the effects of prolonged and excessive stress. Much depends upon the individual condition of course, but the following tips could be helpful:

1. Try to avoid persistently taking on too much work. This is not advice against working hard, but rather against taking on tasks which you suspect that you cannot complete satisfactorily. This tip applies equally to working men and women in all walks of life, to housewives, adolescents and older people.
2. Try to avoid excessive use of drugs of any kind, including alcohol.
3. Make it an absolute rule to take a holiday of some kind, preferably of at least two weeks in length, in every year. Ideally a change of scene is called for, but, when circumstances demand it, a "complete break" at home is better than nothing.
4. Cultivate a hobby or pastime. This prevents obsessive preoccupation with minor personal problems and, in many cases, allows the brain to solve them "unconsciously."
5. Avoid wherever possible situations which you know from past experience are frustrating or irritating. Unnecessary use of the automobile, when public

Rush hours, crowded conditions and noisy machinery make cities a natural breeding ground for stress.

Camera Press

transport will suffice, is a particularly good example of a major stress-inducing habit.

6. Wherever possible try to get as much sleep as you feel you need.

7. Be frank and open in discussing personal problems with members of your family. Many stress problems are unnecessarily inflated by silence, when a half-hour's discussion and conversation can eliminate the source of the problem.

8. Remember that stress only exists when a physical or psychological problem is keeping mind and body on constant if not necessarily high-level alert. In many cases the physical

and psychological problems need only to be identified for them to be removed when the stress will inevitably disappear.

ARE INTELLIGENT PEOPLE MORE LIKELY TO SUFFER FROM STRESS?

There is an old wives' tale which states that highly intelligent people are more likely to go insane than those with only the average complement of brains. There is in fact no evidence to support this belief, but unfortunately there is some element of truth in the faintly similar belief that intelligent people are more likely to suffer from stress. The reason for this is not too difficult to comprehend—intelligent people are more likely to move in a competitive environment, the goals they set for themselves are likely to be more ambitious, and they are also more likely to be aware of the consequences of their failure to achieve these goals. And this is where the intelligent person puts himself at risk; continually alert and striving, he operates in a constant state of high gear. No harm comes of this of course, unless he runs out of nervous energy, or unless for one reason or another he fails to meet the multiple goals he has set his sights on.

CAN YOU BE DRIVEN INSANE THROUGH STRESS?

The difficulty in answering this question is related to the difficulty in

defining "insanity." If the latter is considered to refer to a psychosis—schizophrenia for example—then the answer is probably no. While it was once considered that schizophrenia was a state of psychological withdrawal from insoluble personal conflicts, there is increasing evidence that the psychosis is biochemically determined and not promoted by stressful predicaments themselves. On the other hand, prolonged and severe stress brings in its wake sleeplessness, increasing anxiety and "panicky" states of mind which if not relieved can lead to catastrophic disruptions of mental function which we know by the homely name of "nervous breakdowns." Psychologists and psychiatrists almost invariably can trace the nervous breakdown to the classical pattern of severe stress—a major problem or problems whose solutions elude the afflicted individual.

CAN STRESS AFFECT YOUR DREAMS?

Yes, when you dream, you are processing the information put into the brain in the course of the day, and dreams themselves are part of the mechanism for solving the problems posed in your waking life. Points of stress therefore figure prominently in your dream life, as the psychoanalysts were quick to realize. It is for this reason that psychoanalytic theory involves the patient and the analyst conducting a joint investigation of the former's dream life, for through it can be detected the real origins of conflict and ultimately the origins of stress itself.

HOW DO DRUGS AFFECT STRESS?

It is easy to say that a cure for stress is to remove the barrier that is preventing the individual from reaching his goal and which keeps him in a state of suspended anxiety. But life is not so obliging. If work presents intractable problems, or one's home life is full of discord, it is pointless and irrational to merely wish that the problems would vanish. Chronic stress may be induced with measurable psychological and dangerous physical side effects. Under these circumstances medical practitioners frequently prescribe drugs whose effects are to lower the anxiety associated with stress, restore sleep to a fragmenting mind, and invoke a sense of confidence and well-being which allow the individual to solve his problems afresh. Broadly speaking there are

three types of drugs which act in this way—sedatives, tranquilizers and antidepressants. The sedatives are, basically speaking, sleep-inducers or hypnotics. Some of them have been in use in this role for thousands of years—morphine and alcohol in particular. Newer drugs in this class, and among the most widely used, are barbiturates. These drugs act as depressants of central nervous system activity and as such can do much to remove stress at least temporarily. They have the marked disadvantage of being addictive. The second class, the tranquilizers (e.g. librium, valium, etc.), exert a general calming effect

without however depressing the level of consciousness or alertness, and allow the highly stressed individual to continue working without disruption of his mental sharpness or physical responsiveness. The third class, the antidepressants (e.g. benzedrine, dexedrine, etc.), have a generally stimulating effect rather than purely "lifting" depression. This tends to produce erratic sleep, somewhat eccentric behavior, and the drugs may also be addictive. No set of drugs, incidentally, is without its side effects and their regular use can in the long run only be harmful. People in constant high stress therefore have to balance in some way the merits of "feeling better" against the risk of general drug dependence.

WHAT IS THE BEST TREATMENT FOR STRESS?

There is no treatment in the strict sense of the word. Stress is a natural state which will occur in any situation where the solution to a psychophysical problem lags some way behind its onset. Stress symptoms can be relieved by certain drugs but the stress itself is not removed. Stress may be avoided by cutting down your participation in life but even this is not a complete answer. The simple fact is that stress is an inevitable part of the human condition and will only cease completely when the human brain and body cease to function at death.

Jung: Every symbol has a value

At one time Freud regarded Carl Jung as his natural successor. But later disagreements over the significance of the sexual drive turned their friendship to bitter rivalry.

Jung, the most famous psychologist after Freud, is probably best known for his interests in mysticism—interests that aroused suspicion at the time but which make him distinctly popular today.

Jung believed that man inherits a need to relate to myths and symbols—because they give apparent meaning to life. This need is not a "conscious" one: rather, it exists in us in what psychologists call the unconscious.

The well-adjusted man needs to come to terms with his unconscious, to reconcile it with his conscious mind. All men have common inherited patterns of emotional and mental behavior (what Jung called the archetypes) and these produce fantasies, thoughts and actions that are essentially symbolic.

Increasingly, however, man has been rejecting his unconscious and its useful symbol-creating capacity. Our world has become dehumanized as scientific understanding grows. Because man is no longer involved in

Jung divided human awareness into four functions. He argued that extroverts felt and sensed more than introverts who relied more on thinking and intuition. This natural tendency would determine what symbols arose from the unconscious mind.

nature, he feels himself isolated in the cosmos. Natural phenomena have slowly lost their symbolic implications, he wrote in a popular book completed shortly before his death in 1961, *Man and his Symbols.*

"Thunder is no longer the voice of an angry god, nor is lightning his avenging missile. No river contains a spirit, no tree is the life principle of a man, no snake the embodiment of wisdom, no mountain cave the home of a great demon. No voices now speak to man from stones, plants, and animals, nor does he speak to them believing they can hear. His contact with nature has gone, and with it has gone the profound emotional energy

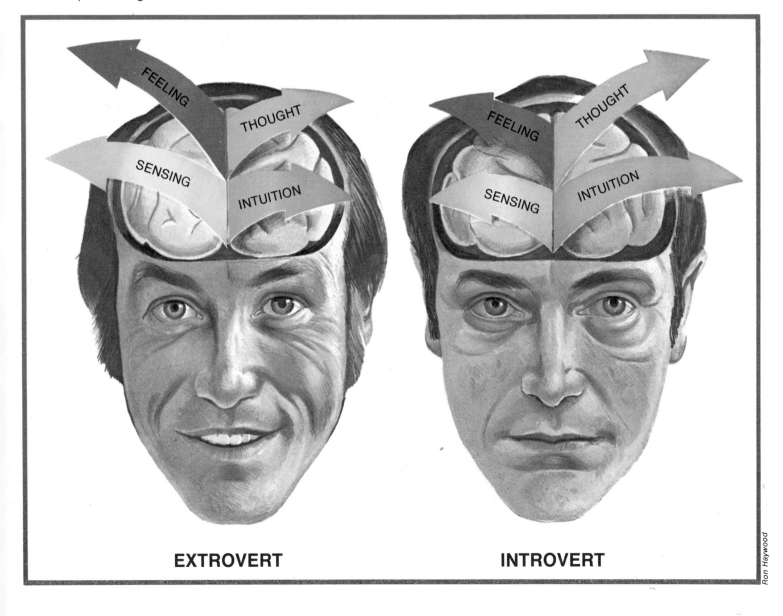

EXTROVERT   INTROVERT

Ron Haywood

that his symbolic connection supplied," said Jung.

He comments that paradoxically we know more *about* mythological symbolism than any generation before our own. But in former times "men did not reflect upon their symbols; they lived them and were unconsciously animated by their meaning."

In modern man the unconscious now expresses itself most freely in dreams. The symbols we encounter in dreams, if we can interpret them, have precise personal significance for the dreamer and should not be dismissed as insignificant. Sometimes these symbols have a "mythological" identity: "We have to take into consideration the face [first observed and commented on by Freud] that elements often occur in a dream that are not individual and that cannot be derived from the dreamer's personal experience." Jung traced similarities between the dream pictures of modern man and the mythological motifs of primitive cultures.

Nature and Mythology

The symbols in our dreams can be compensation for our loss of communication with our unconscious—expressing something the unconscious wanted to say. Frustratingly, though, they express their contents in the language of nature, which is now strange and incomprehensible to us. For this reason, the psychologist who attempts to analyze a patient's dream must have experience not only of dreams and the unconscious but also of mythology.

Power of the Unconscious

In any case, interpretation of dreams is time-consuming and exacting and not to be undertaken lightly. There are no easy reference lists of meanings for different symbols—comforting and entertaining as this might be. A symbol has significance only to the individual dreamer in the individual context. The analyst or therapist must be wary of influencing the patient's slow and uncertain interpretation. "I have made it a rule to remind myself," wrote Jung, "that I can never understand somebody else's dream well enough to interpret it correctly."

Jung's investigation of dreams was very largely based on the dreams of mentally disturbed people—his patients. Many crises in our lives, he pointed out, have a long unconscious history", with the unconscious passing the information to us through our dreams. The message may or may not be benevolent. He cites the case of a

Jung and alchemy

The Rosarium (an alchemical text) says, "Out of man and woman make a round circle and extract a quadrangle and from the quadrangle the triangle. Make a round circle and you will have the philosophers' stone." The modern intellect naturally regards this as poppycock but this ignores the fact that such ideas exist and played an important part for many centuries. It is for psychology to understand *these things*, leaving the layman to rant about poppycock and obscurantism. Many of my critics who call themselves scientific behave exactly like the bishop who excommunicated cockroaches for their unseemly proliferation.

C. G. Jung
Psychology and Alchemy.

Jung discovered that one of the root causes of mental breakdown among his patients was "loss of religious faith." Freud's materialistic outlook offered no solution to this and so Jung began to turn away—as he put it—"from therapy to the art of living." Most of his later studies were concerned with subjects that his colleagues dismissed as "antiquated superstition"—alchemy, astrology and myth.

In addition, Jung himself had personal reasons for this new departure. During a serious illness in 1944, when at death's door, he felt himself pulled out of his body into the heavens only to be recalled by the voice of his visiting physician. From this time Jung dated what he described as "the second and most fruitful half of my long life." Jung was gifted with paranormal powers and demonstrated his power to move objects without touching them to the disbelieving Freud.

Jung believed that alchemy (to most merely an early form of chemistry riddled with mumbo-jumbo) was "a religion rather than a science." He was convinced that alchemical procedures were allegorical instructions for the curing of psychical disorders. Alchemy he saw as an attempt to reconcile in man the two opposing and universal principles—light and dark, yin and yang. To Jung alchemical symbolism was necessary since it was the only means to express the inexpressible. Many of these same allegories were used in dreams by the subconscious to communicate with the conscious mind.

Popperfoto

patient who had been having a series of "shady affairs." Developing a passion for mountain climbing, he began to have dreams in which he fell off a mountain to his death. Jung warned him to take notice of this dream: otherwise, he *would* fall off a mountain. Six months later the man did so. This dream "warning" was not mystical: it was simply an indication that the man was unconsciously inviting such a happening, as a way out of his difficulties. In fact the guide who witnessed the "accident" said that the man seemed almost to step off into space, rather than fall.

Jung wanted people to learn to

Jung's work on dream symbolism had a profound effect on Western artists. The surrealists in particular, by dealing in terms of the irrational, sought to raise the unconscious into an active creative role. The dreamlike unreality of Salvador Dali's *The Persistence of Memory* shocks the spectator into a new awareness of familiar objects and ideas.

relate positively towards the symbols of their "collective unconscious," rather than mistrusting or despising them. Rejection of them may not affect someone while his life runs smoothly, but if suffering occurs, the absence of an acknowledged meaning to life may make the suffering virtually intolerable to most people.

"From time immemorial, men have had ideas about a Supreme Being (one or several) and about the Land of the Hereafter. Only today do they think they can do without such ideas." Narrowing the word religion to his own experience within his own culture, he comments that the psychological doctor is more often consulted by Jews and Protestants than by Catholics—because the Catholic Church still feels responsible for the "care of the soul's welfare."

Some of the workings of the unconscious may be infantile or "pathological"; but others will be a source of positive and creative activity, vital to the growth and development of the mature personality. This was a point of fundamental disagreement between

Jung and Freud. Jung had been a great admirer of Freud (who was nineteen years older), and had indeed collaborated with him for six years. But he grew to detest Freud's more negative attitude towards the unconscious. In 1961 he wrote: "The ideas of Sigmund Freud confirmed for most people the existing contempt for the psyche. Before him it had been merely overlooked and neglected; it has now become a dump for moral refuse."

The Modern Dilemma

It is not always easy to see what Jung wanted Freud's "moral refuse" to be replaced by. He writes with seeming regret of the will power acquired by civilized man, who has learned to do his work efficiently "without having recourse to chanting and drumming to hypnotize him into the state of doing"; who can dispense with a daily prayer for divine aid, and can translate his ideas into action efficiently, "whereas the primitive seems to be hampered at each step by fears, superstitions, and other

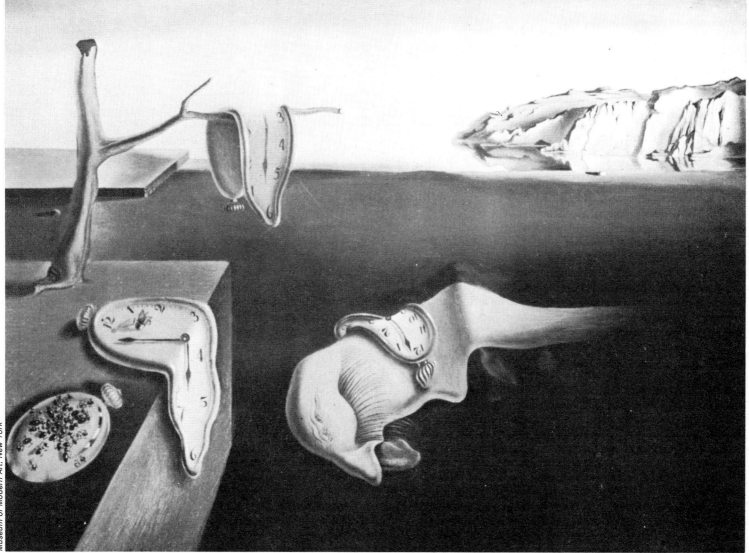

Museum of Modern Art, New York

unseen obstacles to action." Man's gods and demons had not disappeared, but only acquired new names: "They keep him on the run with restlessness, vague apprehensions, psychological complications, an insatiable need for pills, alcohol, tobacco, food — and, above all, a large array of neuroses." The price modern man paid to sustain his creed was "a remarkable lack of introspection."

Jung has in fact been criticized for seeming so greatly to value introspection — relating to ourself and our archetypal images — that he neglects the relative importance of human relationships.

Personal Vision

It is axiomatic that personal experience strongly colors the thinking of psychologists, and Jung's personal background would seem to support this. Born in Switzerland in 1875, he spent most of his childhood as an only child (another child arrived when he was nine), in a rural area where there were no intellectual equals of his own age. His father was a pastor in the Swiss Reformed Church and an oriental and classical scholar.

His enforced solitude, his automatic close contact with such natural phenomena as birth, death and sex, and his association with peasants who shared his interest in the occult all informed his later thinking.

At a time when religious doubts were hardly tolerated, his eventual questioning of religion was made additionally difficult by his professionally religious upbringing. He developed a distrust of women in general, probably as a result of a traumatic experience at the age of three when his mother left home to spend several months in hospital.

Jung regarded his father as reliable but weak; his mother as the dynamic figure. And, as opposed to Freud's more masculine-based psychology, Jung's analytical psychology is based on the maternal, with images of woman as destroyer as well as protector.

Separation from Freud

Jung originally wanted to be an archeologist, but such training was not available close at hand, and his family was too poor to send him away. He chose medicine instead, and was eventually attracted to psychiatry — then in its infancy. After graduation in medicine, he worked as a hospital psychiatrist. He knew Freud's work, but did not meet him until, at the age of thirty-two, he had already had six

Popperfoto

Carl Gustav Jung (1875-1961). With Sigmund Freud, he laid the basis for modern psychiatry. The partnership ended when Jung insisted that the prime motivation of man sprang from the unconscious awareness of archetypal symbols rather than sex.

years' psychiatric experience and had produced original work of his own.

Jung and Freud collaborated for six years, and had a powerful effect upon each other. The reasons for their separation are in some dispute, but although they began from similar points of investigation — analysis of dreams, "free association" tests, etc. — they were certainly working in very different directions. Where Freud tended to interpret all emotionally significant experience as substitutes or derivatives of sex, Jung tended to treat sexuality as just one symbolic element in man.

Jung was writing *Psychology of the Unconscious*, putting forth his own point of view and pointing out the differences between psychoanalysis

and his own "analytical psychology." It was obviously difficult to publish so dissident a theory without breaking with Freud, and by 1913, when the book was published, they had parted company.

The break affected them both deeply. Jung suffered so badly that he began to feel that there was "some psychic disturbance" in him; and eventually he underwent self-analysis. It is likely that Jung came near to having a schizophrenic breakdown in these years, and that only a strong ego and his creative work kept him from total breakdown. Although he rarely referred to his wife, even in his autobiography, he has written that during this time he was anchored to the external world by his wife and five children and by the psychological needs of his patients.

His interpretation of his own mental disturbance influenced his views of his patients. He believed that mental disturbance might be the source or manifestation of creative insight (not unlike the popular modern theories of R. D. Laing on schizophrenics).

Concepts of the Psyche

The end of the period of crisis was marked by the publication of *Psychological Types*, which greatly enhanced his reputation. The rest of his life was devoted to an immense body of writing, while he continued with his private practice, traveling and lectures.

His psychological system is an intricate one, barely touched on here. The collective unconscious is a purely Jungian concept. The terms extrovert and introvert are his, as is archetype. The facade we present to the world he termed the "persona," and the "shadow" is a sort of converse of this. This opposition may be illustrated by "projection" — the strategy by which a person accuses another person of the attitudes he himself holds, e.g. attributing great jealousy to someone, when one is oneself suffering from jealousy. Within the "shadow," each sex has some of the characteristics of its opposite: males have a set of female traits (the anima) and females a masculine set (the animus).

Although his excursions into extensive philosophical and religious fields diverted attention from them, his contributions to psychology are considerable. For the layman, his theories are perhaps more open to misinterpretation than most, especially if read by someone already suffering from an inability to relate to the external world or hysterically attracted to the unconscious.

Words or numbers?

Are you a words or numbers person? Some of us are fast and clever with figures. Many of us find them daunting. Do not be frightened by the sight of these number puzzles; study them carefully and see if you can work out their relationships. Simple arithmetic — adding, subtracting and multiplying — is all you need! If you can work out a household budget you can surely tackle these. Some of you will find them very easy. You have an aptitude for reasoning with figures.

We all handle language successfully but some people excel in verbal reasoning. They find words easy to understand and can express themselves fluently and precisely. If you like to talk and read you may find the verbal puzzles easier to work out. Many people (and most women) are better with words than figures. Try the following puzzles to find where your aptitudes lie.

Your Score

Numbers

1 correct—your number ability is average; 2 correct—you are better than average with numbers; 3 correct—you are very good with numbers.

Words

1 correct—your word ability is average; 2 correct—you are better than average with words; 3 correct—you are probably very good with words.

If your scores are the same for both parts of the test you are equally good with words and numbers. Most people do better on one or the other. If you took longer than three minutes you need a little more practice to speed up your thinking.

Numbers

TIME LIMIT: It is important that you take no longer than three minutes for these three items.

1. Find the missing number

2. Find the missing number

3. Insert the missing numbers

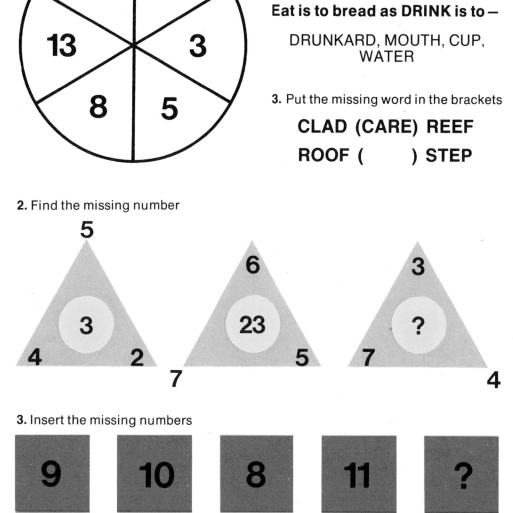

Words

TIME LIMIT: It is important that you take no longer than three minutes for these three items.

1. Find the odd word

ERD BULE LEYWOL VIEF

2. Select the appropriate word

Eat is to bread as DRINK is to—

DRUNKARD, MOUTH, CUP, WATER

3. Put the missing word in the brackets

CLAD (CARE) REEF
ROOF (　　　) STEP

Reg Boorer

Answers—Numbers

1. Add the first number to the next to get the third (5); add the second number to the third to get the fourth number (8); add the third number to the fourth to get the fifth (13); and the fourth to the fifth for the answer (21).

2. Multiply the numbers inside the triangle and subtract from it the number outside the triangle. This gives you the number in the circle. (Answer: 17.)

3. The numbers at the top follow a sequence: +1, −2, +3, −4; those at the bottom: −1, +2, −3, +4. (Answer: 7 over 20.)

Answers—Words

1. The odd word is **VIEF** (five). The

2. The appropriate word is **WATER** — others are all colors (red, blue, yellow).

3. The missing word is **ROSE**. The first and third letters of the word to the left of the bracket make up the first two letters of the missing word; the first and third letters of the word to the right of the bracket add the last two letters of the missing word.

Marshall Cavendish

Falling in love

Love is . . . what? Poets have seen it as "a fever" and "a nightmare living death." Love is moon, June and mascara. Women have pined away for lack of it. Men have killed for it—and sometimes died from it (unrequited passion is thought to be a cause of coronary thrombosis). Is there anything we *can* say with certainty about this tender, but destructive, emotion we call love?

There is very little the scientists can tell us about love. It cannot be examined under a microscope; nor, despite it supposedly being a matter of the heart, can it be diagnosed by a stethoscope. Indeed the strange thing about love, falling into it, out of it, seeking it and perhaps never finding it, is that it appears to be a state of mind, perhaps even enchantment.

At least that is true about "romantic" love, which is all magic, soft music and low lights. And when he says: "Darling, just look at the moon," he is not trying to interest her in astronomy, but hoping instead to overcome her resistance by conjuring up one of love's most potent images.

The Chemistry of Love

But what about "the real thing"? What is it that attracts two people and draws them together? Is there an explanation for the apparently inexplicable chemistry of love and for those aspects of it which do not seem to conform to any kind of logic?

Maybe, by examining one facet of the whole picture, we can throw some light on the question. Let us take, for example, one of the many phenomena with which the state of love and attraction is beset—that of make-up. A woman does not have to be a magician to know that by adding a touch of mascara to her eyes and lipstick to her mouth she is making herself more attractive. But why? And from where did womankind obtain this intuitive know-how?

For there is nothing new in the art of make-up. Women through the ages have been giving nature a helping hand. Ladies of the Roman Empire powdered their faces with white lead. This attempt to play the "femme fatale" was certainly fatal; many of these would-be sirens died of lead poisoning and it is even alleged that

Like this couple, most of us fall into it—out of it—or actively seek love. But what causes that special magic between two people?

this cosmetic catastrophe played its part in the downfall of the great and glorious Roman Empire.

In more recent times the roundabout of fashion has seen a return to such white-faced and dark-eyed looks that it seems difficult to believe that these diseased-looking females belong to the same species, let alone the same sex, as those bronzed bouncing beauties of the swimsuit ads.

But, curiously, it does seem to work. That is why the ladies do it. At first sight there seems no reason why a man should find a floured face more attractive than a florid one. A physician confronted with one of these white-faced creatures with tired-looking eyes might well suspect a serious illness.

First, influenced by the emaciated frame and the bright eyes in their dark surroundings, he might conclude this was a case of tuberculosis. Yet the touch of rouge in the cheeks might sway him towards heart disease. The doll-like splash of red upon the pale cheek bears some resemblance to the malar flush of mitral stenosis.

Grim as it is, students of the heart, whether they be poets or professors of medicine, have always recognized the long-standing association between love, beauty and sickness.

Alexander Dumas had his Lady of the Camelias and William Shakespeare cried out in a sonnet that "my love is a fever, longing still for that which no longer nurses the disease."

Pale and Interesting

Lovers have always been love-sick and, for as long as anyone can remember, hearts have been left bleeding, broken and battered from the ravages of love. After all a condition that is symbolized by an arrow transfixing the heart is clearly serious. And even in these enlightened days doctors do not entirely dismiss the idea that you *can* die from a broken heart. An unhappy love affair may yet be found to be a cause of coronary thrombosis.

This association of love and sick-

ness is further enhanced—if that be the word—by the fact that both may be symbolized by the same pallor. Thus, to Robert Graves, the Love Goddess is eternally the White Goddess and Coleridge wrote with enthusiastic awe: "Her face was white as leprosy, the nightmare living death was she."

It is interesting to note that the ability to recognize and distinguish colors of the spectrum may be relatively recent. Homer enthused over the wine-red Mediterranean and the Greeks often gave their gods blue hair. But as far as red, black and white is concerned there is no evidence of similar confusion. Men always seem to have nursed a soft spot for girls with white faces and love and illness of a kind have always been *traditional*, if unlikely, partners. But why?

Mother Love

The answer to that, and with it one answer as to the nature of love and attraction, lies not, as has already been suggested, in the heart, but in some part of the mind.

And yet, if it *is* the mind, or some powerful yet unconscious memory, that tells a woman she can cast a compelling spell with a white face, then any explanation may come only from psychoanalysis; and the psychoanalysts tell us—rightly or wrongly—that life is one long search to repair the damage inflicted upon us when we were parted from mother's breast.

There, they say, we experienced the kind of peace and contentment that we spend the rest of our lives trying to rediscover. In our search for love and a partner, we are on the lookout for the love that first made so telling an impact upon us—the never-to-be forgotten image of the first love object, mother.

However, what has all that to do with lead powder, white faces and hollow eyes? To answer that we need to imagine how the baby really does see this object of love.

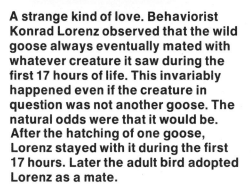

He is a camera, looking out at life through a primitive lens that superimposes an impression of every event upon what he already feels and experiences as a result of his natural instincts. Images from his environment intermingle with his genetic structure to build up a complete personality in the manner of an identikit picture.

At first, because his eyes lack accommodation, he sees only within a narrow field of focus. At a certain distance images fill the screen with a magnificent 3-D giant picture. The image that he sees most often and which makes the most indelible impression at this stage is the image of his mother.

As she enters his field of focus he suddenly sees her face filling the screen and as she moves away it vanishes with equal suddenness. This is magic, this is the fairy godmother, popping in and out of his life as in a fairy tale or a pantomime. It is a performance that he never forgets. Stagestruck, he continues to clamor to see the show again.

Goose Love

Then comes the shock of separation. He is weaned and to console himself he daydreams. He has hallucinations. He imagines he sees his mother's presence at his cotside. Yes, if he tries really hard he can just make out the pale oval of her face and the dark orbs of her eyes. He is still a camera, but the film has gone into reverse, playing back the images that it has faithfully recorded.

The impact that his image of the first love object has upon him is incalculable. Perhaps it should be measured against effects that can be pro-

A strange kind of love. Behaviorist Konrad Lorenz observed that the wild goose always eventually mated with whatever creature it saw during the first 17 hours of life. This invariably happened even if the creature in question was not another goose. The natural odds were that it would be. After the hatching of one goose, Lorenz stayed with it during the first 17 hours. Later the adult bird adopted Lorenz as a mate.

duced upon the sensitized personality of the wild goose.

Konrad Lorenz has carried out some intriguing experiments. Apparently the wild goose will eventually accept as its mate whatever creature it sees within its first 17 hours of life.

Nature, reasonably enough, assumed that the probabilities of that creature being another wild goose were overwhelming. There was nothing to legislate against the intervention of Dr. Lorenz, who took a wild goose and made sure its personality recorded only himself in those critical 17 hours. There were no thunderbolts. Nothing happened until the goose reached maturity. Then the "film" of its personality developed, produced its picture of Dr. Lorenz who was promptly accepted as a desirable mate. Indeed, the goose considered itself a human being and would no doubt have considered mating with its own kind as bestiality.

A wild goose chase, of course, but it makes the point. The lover is also in search of an image—of the pale oval face and the dark eyes which is how he remembers his earliest experiences of his mother. His quest for romance is a journey of rediscovery

in which he seeks the familiar rather than the strange.

As he chases after a mate the image imprinted upon his personality years ago serves as an unconscious signpost. His reactions upon coming face to pale face with one of those dressed-up specters are now more understandable. The fellow thinks he is seeing a ghost and the effect is absolutely paralyzing. In no time at all he is prostrate at her feet, worshipping the white goddess and her unhealthy good looks. After all, show a savage a fluorescent tube and he will probably fall over himself to make obeisance before its ghostly washed-out neon glare.

Face Up to It

A goddess, a ghost, what does it matter? It is the confrontation, in reality, with an image hitherto scarcely glimpsed even in our dreams, but which, like the shutter of a camera, clicks all at once.

It is the dawn of recognition emerging from a long and patient development. There is no such phenomenon as love at first sight in our emotional repertoire. The whole process of courtship is designed to allow the image to develop. A girl needs "time to know her own mind," or, rather, what is in it, for she, just as much as the man, is influenced by images that arise only slowly from the depths of her unconscious.

Invariably the premature proposal meets with a peremptory refusal. Love is a slow developer. You have to give the spell time to work.

So, when a girl paints her face white she is merely giving the chemistry of attraction a helping hand.

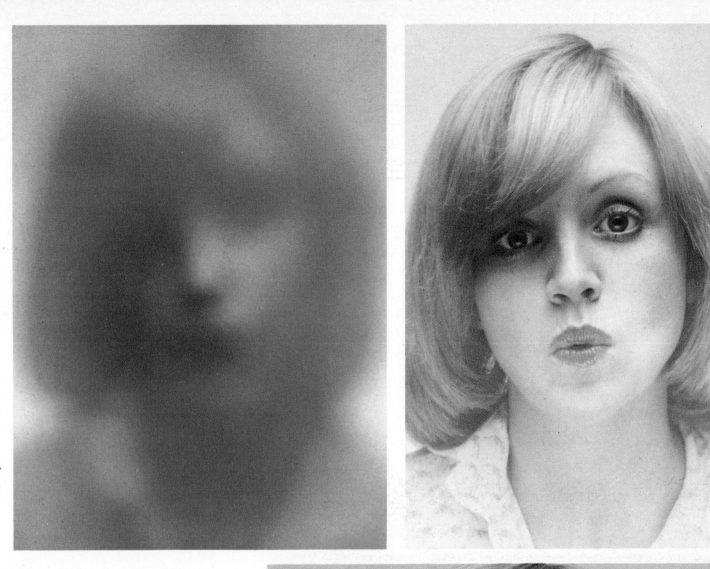

Mother. The sound of this simple word conjures up intensely pleasurable sensations for nearly all of us. To most the memory is of someone who brought us love and peace with her presence. Then came that highly traumatic event — separation from mother — and we were never quite the same again. She was gone. The woman who meant so much became a memory. All of us spend the rest of our lives trying to recapture or recreate with another person the kind of love we had with her. Artists of every kind have obsessively celebrated the image and aura of their mothers. The image (above left) is probably how most babies first see their mother. Then the face is blurred and indistinct. First, only the eyes (top right) stand out in the beloved face; the rest is still indistinct. Finally, the face that is the most important in the world comes into focus (bottom) and the baby beams happily up into it. The adult lover will look for that white oval face and those dark eyes everywhere, whether they are real or merely painted on.

Kim Sayer

The Changing Face of Beauty

The adage that "there's nothing new under the sun" is demonstrably true for aids to beauty. For although motives for applying cosmetics to the face and to the body have varied over the centuries, such practices date back to prehistory. Cave paintings show priests with their bodies painted and in masks to simulate animals. Such body painting acted as camouflage when the wearers went hunting and the cave painting served both as sympathetic magic and as a practical aid in catching animals.

Keeping in the "Pink of Fashion"

But in historic times and in civilized societies the main purpose of painting the face and body is to enhance beauty. Desirable features are emphasized—usually the eyes or the mouth—blemishes are camouflaged and the ravages of age are hidden. The idea is to simulate the bloom of youth or to be "in the pink of fashion." And always, throughout the centuries, there has tended to be an alternation between make-up that is overt, heavy, even excessive to the point of stylization, and that which is subtle, naturalistic, denying that it exists.

In general it is true to say that overt use of make-up has usually coincided with periods of license and sexual freedom, and that those periods when faces were painted with more subtlety and discretion were those of more inhibited manners.

The ancient Egyptians have left vivid records in wall paintings and in tomb furnishings of their make-up habits, and it is remarkable if we look at the cosmetics and beauty aids they used to find how few things we have been able to add to the list.

Nothing New since Cleopatra

They had skin creams of all kinds, rouge, eye shadow, eye liners, a large range of perfumes, solid and essences, and colored foundation creams. They also shaved their heads and wore elaborate wigs, stained their nails, the palms of their hands, and the soles of their feet with henna. And they accented the veins on the temples and the breasts and painted their nipples gold. Cleopatra used black on her brows and lashes, blue-black on her upper lids, and Nile green on her lower lids. (Elizabeth Taylor's make-up as the Queen in the film *Cleopatra* was not exaggerated.) It was a highly stylized work of art, designed to emphasize Cleopatra's divinity.

To a lesser extent this was true of the make-up used by Queen Elizabeth I. She used red and white paint thickly on all her exposed skin and the older she grew, the thicker the layers became. Her portraits show a mask of sovereignty, not the face of a woman, and this is not due entirely to the style of portrait painting of the day. After she started to age, it is said that Elizabeth would never look at herself in a looking glass; perhaps she looked instead at her portraits, which still showed her what she wanted to see.

The elaborate, stylized make-ups designed to set persons apart have one defect: they can readily be copied by lesser beings. And though sumptuary laws and taxes might be passed and imposed to attempt to limit excesses in adornment, and though nobles might frown and churchmen rail it has usually been found impossible to restrict fashion, including make-up, to the élite. Men and women always find a way of joining in the fashionable swim. For example, in Elizabeth's time red hair became all the rage, and recipes for dying the hair all shades of red, like the Queen's, abounded. Now fashions run their race in a matter of months rather than years.

In Tune, but Tortured

Green nails and spangled eyelids are seen on a pop star one day, designed to give him a bit of his own mystique and set him apart from all the other pop stars. The next day all the fans are demanding green nail varnish and spangles for their eyelids—and the next week the manufacturers have rushed products onto the market to catch the fashion.

The tortures that women are prepared to suffer in order to achieve the current idea of beauty have often been noted by sociologists. They include tight lacing, which led to malformation of the rib cage and crushing of the organs within the diaphragm; the binding of feet by the Chinese and Japanese, which made normal walking impossible; and tattooing. Also, the piercing of ear lobes and the septum of the nose to permit the wearing of jewels; the plucking of hair from brows, temples and the forehead; and the filing of teeth.

Many women have died in pursuit of a white complexion, through the concoctions of white lead and mercury salts which they have used for their enameling, despite clear warnings from doctors for hundreds of years. Both are cumulative poisons, with extremely nasty effects both on the appearance and the health of anyone who dares to use them often.

One treatment was used to remove the entire skin of the face with oil of vitriol or mercury water, in the fond hope that the replacement skin would be an improvement on the old.

Women today do not go to such lengths, and indeed are better informed by doctors as to the structure of their skin and the true results of such practices. But they do still willingly go to considerable pains to improve their appearance—for example, from electrolytic or wax depilation and from cosmetic surgery.

Strange Recipes for the Face

But though modern seekers after beauty may be prepared to endure discomfort in pursuit of their ideal, some of the recipes prescribed by the ancients would almost certainly turn their stomachs. One Egyptian hair dye was made of the blood of a black cow, tortoise shell and the neck of a gabeu bird. Other ingredients of ancient beauty preparations included horn of fawn, bile of crabs, dried tadpoles, womb of cat, date blossoms and asses' hooves. A most effective mud pack was made from crocodile's excrement—dried. Shakespeare's Weird Sisters and their cauldron had nothing on this.

Nowadays, we are on a back-to-nature kick—everything has to be "pure" and "fresh" and "made from natural ingredients." All well and good, but let us not think this is new either. Throughout the centuries homemade beauty preparations have included natural ingredients such as lemons, egg white, flower and fruit decoctions, and the water in which various pulses, such as beans or barley, have been boiled.

Hamlet, in pettish mood, remarked to Ophelia that "God gives you one face and you make yourselves another." So it was then, so it is still; and we make ourselves the face that is the pleasing image of our time.

Beauty is an odd business. It is also big business, and has been so for some time. Even Madame Pompadour —whose last act before she fell asleep and died was to rouge her face— spent more than $100,000 on perfume alone, as long ago as the eighteenth century. By 1930 American women spent at least $2,000 million on their skin, or more than the total budgets of half a dozen states. Nor are the men lagging behind: in 1963 a new, exotic man's cologne called Jade East sold $700,000 worth in the first six months.

Chris Walter

Camera Press

Three examples of how make-up can be used to highlight the human face. At bottom is Queen Elizabeth I, who painted her skin a thick red and white. Top left is David Bowie, a British pop star who uses make-up to add to his mystique. On the right is a Geisha girl with a carefully contrived white face designed to enhance her beauty.

Popperfoto

107

All you want to know about...

psychotherapy

Mary Evans

Q WHO INVENTED PSYCHO-THERAPY?

A No one invented it. It has gradually evolved from the moment when people realized that there could be disorders of the emotions or the "spirit" as well as those of the organic body. As long as 2500 years ago Hippocrates, who is reckoned to be the father of medicine, seems to have realized that promoting bodily well-being and mental tranquility might often be beneficial to people suffering from emotional disorders but his attitude was an unusual one. Early theories assumed that disorders of the mind or spirit were due to invasion or attack by evil forces of one kind or another. What we would today term neurotic behaviour was

thought to be caused by witchcraft of some kind, while the major psychoses were attributed to possession by devils. The most logical "therapy" therefore would be to make life as unpleasant as possible for the invading spirits, with the result that the mentally ill were often beaten or tortured, and occasionally put to death. The practice of chaining the insane—no doubt to keep them from harming themselves and others as much as anything else—continued until the end of the eighteenth century, when the first signs of general enlightenment came with the great French reformist Philippe Pinel, who symbolically unchained the inmates of the main Parisian lunatic asylum. Pinel had no clear theory of mental illness though, and psychotherapy proper

Electro-convulsive therapy (ECT) was once widely used. Today it is an uncommon and controversial treatment for schizophrenia and acute depression.

could not get underway until a theory was developed. It is now generally agreed that the first such theory, and indeed the origins of a world revolution in the understanding and treatment of mental illness, came in the latter half of the nineteenth century with the great insights of the Austrian physician Sigmund Freud. Freud's genius introduced the theory of *psychoanalysis*, one of the most powerful approaches to understanding mental illness, and to this extent he can be considered as the father of psychotherapy, if not its inventor.

WHAT IS PSYCHOTHERAPY?

A literal translation is "cure or treatment of the mind," and as a working definition this will do. Technically speaking it should therefore embrace all the various kinds of treatments which are employed in dealing with mental illnesses, great and small, and which might vary from mild depression right up to the most extreme forms of psychosis. By modern convention however, psychotherapy has come to imply all those forms of treatment in which the principal therapeutic tool is a verbal exchange between a doctor or other specialist and his patient or patients. Forms of treatment which principally involve the use of drugs, "electric shock treatment" or, in extreme cases, psychosurgery, are *not* generally classed as psychotherapy, though its course may be assisted from time to time by the occasional use of drug or shock therapy. Since it is generally assumed that there are two separate, though occasionally overlapping, causes of mental disorders—the psychological (for example, severe depression due to marital problems) and the physiological (psychotic behavior caused by a brain malfunction), it would seem reasonable to treat the psychological disturbance by psychological means, and the remainder by physiological means. One method or set of methods, for the sake of simplicity, we tend to assign to psychotherapy, the remainder to psychiatric medicine. While the dividing line between the two is occasionally blurred and both may contain common elements, the distinction is sufficiently important to be made.

WHY DO SOME PEOPLE HAVE PSYCHOTHERAPY WHEN THERE IS APPARENTLY NOTHING WRONG WITH THEM?

Since therapy means treatment it would at first seem pointless for anyone to undergo psychotherapy unless there is something the matter with him! The problem is not so simple as it seems—there is no individual on earth who is perfectly adjusted to the highly complex environment in which he lives, and who is capable of handling all the trials and stresses that life provides. At some stage in our lives we all could benefit by at least supportive psychotherapy, and frequently we get this without actually going to see a psychologist, by "talking things over" with a friend or a member of the family. Beyond all this there is one major area where psychotherapy is given, not with the prime goal of easing a troubled mind, and this is in the area of training therapists themselves. This particularly applies in the case of psychoanalysis. Freud, while qualified in medicine himself, always believed that psychoanalysis could be practiced with 100 percent success by non-medically qualified individuals—provided that they had undergone psychoanalysis themselves. Thus "training analysis," as it is called, served principally to instruct the would-be professional in the skills and insights of analysis, with the restructuring of his personality as a secondary rather than a principal goal. Most professional psychoanalysts, incidentally, believe that the restructuring of their personality has been enormously beneficial.

DOES ONE HAVE TO BE A PSYCHOLOGIST TO PRACTICE PSYCHOTHERAPY?

People asking this question are often puzzled at the way in which words like psychologist, psychoanalyst, psychiatrist, etc. are apparently used interchangeably, and wonder whether they have different meanings. The answer is that they do and before attempting to deal with the question as to who is allowed to practice psychotherapy, one needs to get the terms clearly sorted out.

1. *Psychologist:* Psychology is the study of the mind and human behavior. A psychologist is interested in the way the mind works and why it works in that way. He will be interested in "normal" as well as "abnormal" behavior, but he will not necessarily be concerned, or even trained, in the treatment of mental illness. In most countries, in order to practice the treatment of mental disorders or illness, he will need to take some specialist training as a part of his psychological qualifications.

2. *Psychiatrist:* Psychiatry is the science of the treatment of mental illness using specialist techniques which are part of orthodox medicine. A psychiatrist is a name which refers specifically to a doctor of medicine who has taken special courses in the treatment of mental illness. Anyone prescribing drugs or performing surgery in the course of such treatment must be medically qualified.

3. *Psychotherapist:* A psychotherapist is a blanket name given to anyone, whether medically qualified or not, who is qualified to treat people suffering from mental illness. He may be trained merely to give supportive therapy or reconstructive therapy, to individuals or to groups. If he wishes to prescribe drugs however he must be medically qualified.

4. *Psychoanalyst:* A psychoanalyst is someone treating mental illness through the reconstructive techniques developed by Freud and elaborated by some of his followers. He need not necessarily be a psychiatrist, provided that he does not prescribe drugs or perform surgery.

It will be seen that there is some overlap between each and all of the four terms used above. Technically speaking all four fall within the branch of psychology (the study of the mind) and therefore anyone practicing psychotherapy will clearly be a psychologist. In some countries of the world it is in fact illegal to practice psychotherapy for reward unless one is medically qualified (in other words unless one is a psychiatrist). Such regulations, however, greatly reduce the number of people permitted to tackle the enormous contemporary problem of mental illness, and in most countries the law only requires that psychotherapy for reward should be undertaken only by people "suitably" but not necessarily medically trained.

WHAT OTHER PROFESSIONS ARE INVOLVED IN PSYCHOTHERAPY?

Strictly speaking psychotherapy is the province of the psychologist or the psychiatrist, but the very widespread instance of mental disorder, particularly of the milder kind meriting supportive psychotherapy, has led to the deliberate involvement of professions whose role in society is in some ways akin to that of the psychologist. The trend is perhaps most widely developed through the increasing practice of "pastoral counseling," where a minister of religion often stands in the role of psychotherapist. The role of the priest or cleric in giving guidance and easing troubled minds is of course a classic one, and there are many who have pointed to the similarities between the "confessional" of the Roman Catholic Church and the uninhibited display of confidences that occurs in psychoanalysis. In a modern society which maintains strong ties with orthodox religions, the part played by a priest or cleric in counseling and supportive psychotherapy can obviously be a considerable one. Many clergymen, incidentally, go so far as to take courses in psychology to give extra depth and strenth to their counseling role. In many cases this dual function offers the very restrained and over-anxious patient an opportunity to unburden himself of his problems—which after all is essentially the first stage in any successful treatment by psychotherapy.

HOW CAN DRUGS BE USEFUL IN PSYCHOTHERAPY?

Drugs may be used as an adjunct to psychotherapy when they are prescribed by a qualified physician. They have three principal roles:

1. To relieve symptoms and help give some immediate feedback to a patient coming for treatment. In this group the tranquilizers are principally employed to facilitate treatment.

2. As relaxants and anxiety reducers in the course of treatment, with the aim of allowing the individual to think of and speak of his conflicts and problems in an uninhibited fashion, and without undue stress. Here the central nervous system depressants or hypnotics (such as the barbiturates) may be used sparingly to produce a relaxed and slightly euphoric frame of mind in the patient.

3. In certain cases as a stimulant to mental processes and to untap bottled-up or repressed material. In this case psychiatrists have experimented with some hallucinogenic drugs—LSD in particular—because of the bizarre thought processes which they induce and which are reminiscent of schizophrenic thought patterns. Their use in this context is controversial, and LSD therapy is now avoided.

WHAT TYPES OF MENTAL ILLNESS RESPOND SUCCESSFULLY TO PSYCHOTHERAPY?

Any illness which allows the supportive approach. These include simple depressions, anxieties, and phobias; sleep problems; and social, work and family adjustment conflicts. These are the situations in which the therapist can often work wonders by simply indicating that he understands the nature of the problem, can sympathize with it, and can assure the sufferer that his condition is not unique. Listening alone may be enough to alleviate the burden of a problem. People suffering from one or other of these complaints have often lost the will to attempt to deal with them or have fallen into a state of despair and hopelessness. In these cases the psychologist helps to sort out their internal confusion and to provide new motivation and purpose to their lives.

Mary Evans

Charcot's vibration therapy was used on the insane in the 1890s. The cap, powered by an electric motor (right), caused the head to shake violently. It was held on by metal straps (left).

IS ELECTRIC SHOCK TREATMENT PART OF PSYCHOTHERAPY?

It may occasionally be given as an adjunct to psychotherapy, and its particular strength has been found in the relief of severe depression. It is really part of psychiatric medicine. In ECT (the abbreviation for the slightly alarming phrase, electro-convulsive therapy), a brief electric current is passed through the brain by electrodes attached to the scalp. The patient is unconscious and sedated before the current is passed through, and the process is not painful or psychologically unsettling to the great majority of individuals. The most unsettling effect is a period of amnesia, generally of a few minutes only in length, which

surrounds the treatment. Its great role in psychotherapy is to lift the severely depressed patient out of his melancholia so that, with his improved self-confidence, heightened motivation, and a greater interest in his own well-being, he can assist the therapist in the two-way partnership which is known as psychotherapy.

COULD PSYCHOTHERAPY BE USEFUL IN BREAKING BAD HABITS?

It depends what is meant by "bad habits." Giving up smoking, nail biting, blushing, etc. tend to fall more into the camp of the do-it-yourself psychology merchants who advertise in weekly magazines. Nevertheless if the habit is so bad as to be compulsive and is damaging the individual's psychological or physical well-being, then skilled therapy may be useful, not by breaking the habit as such, but by attacking the conflicts or difficulties which lie behind the habit.

WHAT IS THE DIFFERENCE BETWEEN PSYCHOTHERAPY AND PSYCHOANALYSIS?

Psychoanalysis is a *branch* or *approach* to psychotherapy, and it refers to the ideas and techniques of Freud. Its richness and fertility as a source of understanding the dynamics of mental life are such that it merits discussion entirely on its own. In sum, however, psychoanalysis is based on the notion that man is frequently controlled by powerful forces whose existence are not known to the conscious mind, and which may frequently conflict with his consciously expressed wishes and desires. Mental illness is evidence of the battle being raged between conscious and unconscious forces, and this conflict may lead to severe disruption of the personality. Psychoanalysis is a specialist technique which allows the individual, with the guidance and insight of the psychoanalyst, to explore his unconscious, observe the submerged or repressed motives, and thus help to resolve the conflict between the two layers of his mind. Even so it is still only one of a number of approaches to *psychotherapy*, for some of Freud's students and followers—Jung and Adler in particular—broke away to form their own approaches to psychoanalysis, with varying degrees of success. While the Freudian approach is considered to have limitations, it is nevertheless still reckoned to be the most significant model of mental life that has been developed.

B.P.C.

Who pecks whom?

In every hen run there is a top hen who has the right to peck all the other hens without being pecked back. The same pattern is repeated in societies as diverse as those of squirrels, monkeys, even man himself. How do you rate in your community? Are you a top hen, one of the five percent of dominant men and women . . . or just a self-effacing strop for everyone's razor?

We all know from experience that people are not born equal and that there are tremendous differences between individuals. A scale of personality characteristics would show how unequal we are. At the top would be the leaders or those who possess dominance and at the opposite end would be an equivalent number of persons who are happy to be led. In the middle of the scale would be the vast majority, some 90 percent of us, who would all have a position at some point along the line.

The Dominant Sex

What makes one man or one woman dominant over another is still something of a mystery. For instance, we do not understand the nature of that blend of leadership and personal magnetism invariably shown by the truly dominant person. Despite the puzzles

that remain to be solved — and, after all, every aspect of the personality, every facet of psychology is fraught with riddles — we already know a great deal about dominance.

We know that approximately one in twenty people — whether men or women — are dominant personalities, though men tend to show greater dominance than women overall. This distribution of five percent stays remarkably constant in every tribe and civilization. It stays the same in all kinds of different situations. And the same balance exists between the top dogs and the underlings in the animal kingdom — among creatures as different as the hen, the monkey and the squirrel.

In all these groups a hierarchy exists which is recognized and adhered to by all members of the group. The one at the top is acknowledged as domi-

nant and the others follow down the line in a prescribed order. This is seen most clearly in the now famous pecking order among hens. The hen at the top is allowed to peck all those beneath her at will but none of the others are allowed to return the compliment. However, the hen immediately below her can peck everyone else except number one. The poor creature at the bottom must take the brunt of everyone else's aggression yet she is allowed to peck no one in return.

The Self-Made Man

This example provides a good, basic model of the way hierarchies work, and that is how human societies would function if the natural behavioral pattern were not obscured by social systems, class structures and so on. In other words if human beings were put together on a desert island they

Camera Press

would behave according to natural dominance like the hens and not according to which person was in a superior position back home.

We often put people into dominant positions they do not merit because of parents, class or the kind of education they have had. It is important therefore not to think of the dominant person automatically as the one who has a high position, but to look for the dominant personality. All self-made men, because of the initiative they show, fall into this category.

Dominance – the Recipe for Success

How can we define dominance? Most dominant people are intelligent – but although brains certainly help to put you in top positions they are not absolutely essential – instead, a lot of other less obvious qualifications are required. Initiative is one which has already been mentioned.

Many people feel that physical strength is the next most important characteristic in accordance with the old dictum that brawn and brains are an infallible recipe for success. Again, physical strength can help – but it is not crucial. Many a tough, strong and intelligent man is not particularly dominant at all although at first sight he might appear so. Closer acquaintance will show that he lacks that indefinable "something" that the truly dominant person has. It is the indefinable qualities of the personality that really make a person dominant, that make everyone around him single him out and respect him. It is a type of personal magnetism, a charisma, that makes others want to stay with him, drink with him and that makes his followers take notice of everything he says. He is the type that everyone congregates around in the bar, the guy who is automatically followed by

Three individuals who stand out in a crowd. They are examples of the one in twenty persons who are dominant in our society. More often men, they may show their dominant personalities in appearance and behavior.

the rest if he decides to go and sit in another bar.

Such a dominant character is certain to have two assets among all the others – ample self-confidence and a steady gaze. He may have nothing else to offer but if he can remain sure of himself and let you know it by staring you straight in the eye he will automatically intimidate you – without your realizing it – and put you in a subordinate position – unless of course you can give as good as or better than you got.

People are attracted to the dominant member of the group and up to a point they fear him. As a result he does not

The Russian holy man Grigori Rasputin (1871-1916), an historical example of the dominant personality. Of peasant origin, Rasputin had great influence over Czar Nicholas II and the Czarina, Alexandra. This was largely because of his mysterious ability to stop the bleeding of their son, Alexis, who suffered from hemophilia. Said to possess second sight and the power to heal the sick, his gaze could mesmerize.

Mary Evans

need to lift his little finger—without any effort he naturally stays on top. Psychologists have tried for a long time to work out what qualities the dominant man has which give him his great self-confidence. Their research results have enabled them to list a few, such as strength, intelligence, maleness, courage, health, indefinable persistence, and ambition. Another factor is luck which is probably quite important and something that we have no idea how to measure as yet, and perhaps never will.

One in Every Twenty

Having all these qualities he is able to face a multitude of different situations and come out of all of them relatively unscathed. Whatever jam he gets into he is confident he can get out of it—because he has such a variety of strengths to fall back on. He assumes that his health will not suddenly let him down, a possibility some individuals fear greatly; he is certain his wits will not desert him at the crucial moment and that he will remain calm under stress. It is, therefore, the ability to face any situation that gives him that vital confidence.

It is, as a result, the combination of very different qualities all adding up to a rounded whole that forms the essential secret ingredient. We are all born with a combination of different strengths and weaknesses. The person who becomes dominant is born with that particular brand of strengths which allows him virtually complete protection against all attacks—whether they are psychological or physical in nature.

The dominant person is not as vulnerable as others; he has great stability. And it is this type of personality that seems to occur in approximately one in twenty individuals. It occurs in men and women but the added factor of maleness tends to provide an extra boost so that male dominance is of a higher, more aggressive order. This will be demonstrated later through research results. From this account it can be seen that it is personality, rather than ability per se, which makes for dominance.

Another characteristic of the dominant, which has not been mentioned so far but adds up to this picture of the rounded individual able to cope with any situation, is political skill. Another word for it would be tact, or it could be described as the ability to compromise. It involves basically a capacity to get along with one's fellows—not only when things are running smoothly but also in a crisis so that everyone can emerge from this crisis with some sort of order and their relationships still intact. This is particularly important when large groups of people are involved.

The truly dominant person also appears able to suppress his own individualism for the sake of the group as a whole. He is so concerned with his responsibilities as a leader that he can forget himself and his own special needs for a time.

Who will be the Boss?

These remarks all apply to that elusive quality of dominance—but of course not all dominant people are the same—some are much more dominant than others—and some individuals are only mildly so. Just how dominant a person is depends on how much he is allowed to be. For instance, a really dominant individual may never realize his true potential if he is working in a large corporation where there is only one boss. His natural dominance is frustrated—but because it must find expression it will lead into other avenues, possibly into petty crime or beating his wife. On the other hand if he is only mildly dominant he may find that running the local Boy Scouts or organizing golf club meetings satisfies sufficiently his natural dominant streak.

In the past it used to be said that dominance always establishes itself when two animals or human beings pursue the same goal, whether it is for the same job, the same house or the same rabbit warren. One wins and becomes dominant in all things. But psychologists now realize that things are not quite so simple. One man may be the boss in the office and a very good boss too, while his wife rules the roost completely at home.

One of the best writers on the subject of dominance, Robert Ardrey, in his book *The Social Contract,* expresses it like this: "Dominance has long been described as what happens when any two animals pursue the same goal; one succeeds in establishing the dominant relation, the other becomes the subordinate and the relationship will determine without further quarreling all other rivalries. But in our most recent studies animal behavior comes to appear ever more complicated, ever more resembling our own. Just as a man may be dominant in his home, subordinate in his office, popular at the corner bar and a rank-and-filer in the local political organization, so role plays a part in the life of the social animals. The clearly dominant monkey may leave to another leadership of the group in its foraging for food, may lead or not lead a general territorial battle, tolerate without interference the sexual activities of a subordinate and leave to others the chasing off of strangers."

Psychologists use the word "alpha" to describe the dominant individual. Alpha is the first letter, the A of the Greek alphabet. The Greek letter B is beta, C is gamma and so on. Right at the bottom of the scale comes omega. It is easier to mention alphas than to talk continually about the dominant person. Also this classification makes it possible to discuss the relationships of top people with those individuals just below them—the betas (Bs) and so on.

As we have said before—one in twenty of the population are potential alphas. This means that they have all the basic characteristics of alphas—but sometimes these aspirations can be thwarted. In a truly equal society all men and women have equal opportunities and all the alphas automatically rise to the top. This always happens in animal societies where there is no such thing as lack of education, lack of opportunity, inherited privilege and so on.

Keeping a Good Man Down

In human societies, however, many top positions are conferred on non-dominant people just because they have the right connections, and the ones who should be at the top are often kept down because of the deprived conditions into which they were born. This clearly leads to trouble; the true alphas are forced to obey men above them they cannot respect, men who have no real leadership abilities—a situation that the true alpha finds extremely frustrating. This state of affairs is bound to lead to trouble and social instability as the alphas twist and turn to find an outlet.

In order to keep society on an even keel the dominant person must have an opportunity to show himself, to fulfill himself—reach the top. This of course always happens among animals and it creates a very stable community.

The hierarchy that results prevents any fighting, it allows the individuals to know where they are without any bickering, and they are satisfied with their place. Once two human beings know each other and how they stand towards each other they can automatically adjust—without thinking about it—to any new situations that arise. This occurs because of the minor skirmishes that inevitably take place at the beginning stages of any relationship.

The Human Pecking Order

For instance, a new recruit to the office is tested—ever so gently—by all those on the same level to see how he reacts and to see where they should place him in their own scale of things. The battle could involve trivia such as who has which chair, who uses which pencil, but the actions all have symbolic significance.

This kind of battle only occurs between individuals at the same level. There is no point trying to pit one's wits against a boss who has the upper hand by virtue of his position—not at any rate inside the office. In the bar different rules operate and a much finer indication of which personalities are really dominant emerges.

Now the people with whom you do battle are different—but again they are equals in that particular situation. You might try to establish supremacy with a beta if you are an alpha but with individuals below that point you will remain aloof. Similarly someone who is a non-dominant personality will struggle only with others on the same level of dominance or at any rate very close to it. It is the same in the animal world. Two stags will fight only if they are equals. For a long time they will size each other up, then either move off or fight. And it has been observed that the stags base their final decision on psychological factors rather than physical ones.

The Shepherds and the Sheep

Hierarchy is in fact very important in any group organization where individuals of unequal abilities have to settle down and coexist together—it reduces the need for struggle and fighting.

Basically we are all—wherever we are in this hierarchy—striving constantly to fulfill ourselves, to climb upwards on the social scale. We all want to be dominant personalities to some extent. However, if we were all

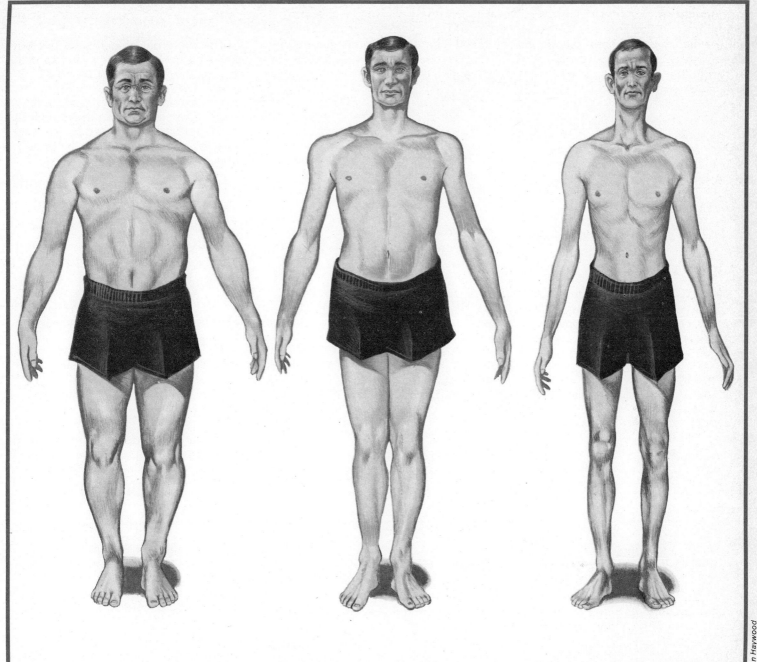

Ron Haywood

dominant, chaos would result—there would be total anarchy. And indeed in some societies where the alphas are kept down by artificial means anarchy can become a real danger. But fortunately the people who are genuinely low on the dominance scale are quite happy to be followers in most things.

These subordinates take pleasure in following, they watch and listen for and then copy the words and actions of the dominants. They learn from these leaders and the views of the leaders become part and parcel of the general culture. But they do not expect dominants to learn anything from them and if it does happen it occurs very slowly.

Experiments with monkeys in Japan have shown that if an omega invents

A psychologist has shown that physique and character are related. Most people are to some degree of three basic types. They are (from left to right) the endomorph, the mesomorph, and the ectomorph. The endomorph is usually of soft and chubby appearance, the mesomorph of hard and rectangular build, while the ectomorph is thin and fragile. A person's build often determines his behavior, habits, and interests: a dominant individual is usually an energetic, vital mesomorph.

something new the information spreads very slowly if at all. If on the other hand a firebrand alpha makes a discovery the knowledge is transmitted very quickly to everyone except the very old of the group.

The same force that compels the alphas to dominate makes others accept willingly a lesser lot. There is what is described by the psychologist Wynne-Edwards as "a hereditary compulsion to comply."

Besides our upward striving, human beings—as well as other animals—have the opposite quality, a readiness to accept whatever happens to be our station in life, a willingness to accept subordination.

Not only are some people quite content with an inferior station in life, some actually welcome and enjoy it. The personality of the dominant fascinates them: we have only to look at the cult followings of movie idols or even politicians to realize the overwhelming impact of the dominant personality.

Test your vocabulary

The English language is one of the richest in the world yet in everyday conversation we use just a fraction of our potential word power. Language enriches communication, makes us more aware of experience. Words can persuade, describe, fascinate. Can you go beyond the limits of common-place words? Test your vocabulary. You may know more than you think. From this exercise, you can learn to extend your command of the spoken and written word.

There is a time limit of 30 minutes.

Word Meanings

From each group of six words below, write the word you believe is *nearest in meaning* to the word in heavy black type above it.

1. DEVIOUS
Difficult, contrasting, prying, indirect, stealthy, dividing.

2. INFAMOUS
Hostile, notorious, humble, respected, friendly, childish.

3. PROCRASTINATE
Support, pretend, dispute, delay, postulate, demean.

4. MOMENTOUS
Transitory, small, large, joyful, unanimous, important.

5. MITIGATE
Help, excuse, condemn, alleviate, explain, release.

6. SAGACIOUS
Fine, wise, traditional, herbal, elderly, talkative.

7. RECUMBENT
Duty, burden, reclining, mountain, successor, rising.

8. PARSIMONIOUS
Vegetable, clerical, hypocritical, poor, stingy, harmonious.

9. ESTRANGE
Alienate, exotic, far-reaching, divorce, unknown, exchange.

10. LIBERTINE
Anarchist, profligate, rescuer, missionary, pacifist, bookworm.

Same or Opposite

Do these words mean the same, or nearly the same; or do they mean the opposite? Record your answers (Same or Opposite) on a separate sheet of paper.

1. Permanent — Transitory
2. Inimitable — Unique
3. Melancholy — Hilarity
4. Sated — Replete
5. Favorable — Propitious
6. Rigid — Flexible
7. Enmity — Animosity
8. Recalcitrant — Malleable
9. Slanting — Oblique
10. Truthful — Candid

Word Building

How many words of four letters or more (no plurals, proper names or foreign words) can you make from

ERRONEOUS

Answers

Word Meanings

1. **DEVIOUS:** Indirect, not straightforward; as in "a *devious* chess player."

2. **INFAMOUS:** Notorious, of ill-fame; as in "the *infamous* highwayman."

3. **PROCRASTINATE:** Delay, put off, postpone; as in "*procrastinating* on a decision."

4. **MOMENTOUS:** Important, weighty; as in "a *momentous* occasion."

5. **MITIGATE:** Alleviate, appease, reduce severity of; as in "*mitigating* circumstances." (Law)

6. **SAGACIOUS:** Wise, judicious; as in "*sagacious* with age."

7. **RECUMBENT:** Reclining, lying down; as in "*recumbent* on the grass."

8. **PARSIMONIOUS:** Stingy, miserly; as in "*parsimonious* Old Scrooge."

9. **ESTRANGE:** Alienate, to make indifferent in feeling, as in "*estranged* from his family."

10. **LIBERTINE:** Profligate, a debauchee, a licentious or dissolute man; as in "the *libertine* Casanova."

Same or Opposite

1. OPPOSITE
2. SAME
3. OPPOSITE
4. SAME
5. SAME
6. OPPOSITE
7. SAME
8. OPPOSITE
9. SAME
10. SAME

Word Building

We found 20 familiar words: ROSE, RUNE, RUSE, ROUSE, SOON, SORE, SURE, SNORE, SEEN, SEER, SNEER, SOUR, ENSURE, ENSUE, ONUS, ONEROUS, OURS, USER, NOSE, NOOSE.

Wordpower

Though the English language contains about 490,000 words as well as 300,000 technical terms—the most in any language—it is doubtful if any individual uses more than 60,000. An educated person tends to use about 5,000 words in speech and 10,000 words when writing but the average vocabulary is only between 1-2,000 words. Shakespeare, on the other hand, used about 21,000 different words in all his plays.

Scoring

Word Meanings

- 10—excellent
- 7-9—very good
- 5-6—good
- under 5—average to poor

Same or Opposite

- over 20—excellent
- 16-20—very good
- 10-15—good
- under 10—average to poor

Word Building

World Medicine

Masters & Johnson
Seeing's believing

Sex is a natural birthright. Yet it is only since World War II that uninhibited research has begun to give us a deep and genuine understanding of one of life's most exciting pleasures.

When, and if, the definitive volume on the psychology, physiology and practice of sex is ever written, the work of Dr. William Masters and Mrs. Virginia Johnson will undoubtedly form a major contribution.

In 1948 and 1953 Dr. Alfred Kinsey's studies had rocked America, revealing an astounding disparity between accepted attitudes towards sexual behavior and actual sexual practice. But these findings were based on interviews with volunteers and were therefore subjective. Almost all the data was secondhand, and Dr. Kinsey himself was acutely aware of the need for direct scientific observations and records of sexual responses. He was making plans to follow through with research on these lines when he died in 1956.

Masters' and Johnson's two books, *Human Sexual Response,* published in 1966, and *Human Sexual Inadequacy* four years later, carried on where Dr. Kinsey left off. They were based on direct observations made in the laboratory and recorded on film the sexual activities, including intercourse, masturbation and artificial coition, of nearly 700 men and women. They treated these activities in exactly the same way as digestion or respiration, i.e. as a biological function.

Masters – a Solid Reputation

William Howell Masters was born in Cleveland in 1915 and graduated in science from Hamilton College in Clinton, New York, in 1938. The following year he entered the University of Rochester School of Medicine and Dentistry, where he worked for the anatomist Dr. George Washington Corner on the relationship between the human menstrual cycle and the estrous cycle in infra human animals.

By 1942 Masters' interest focused on researching human sexual behavior; this was at that time a field obviously wide open for investigation and public opinion was just about ready to accept the need for it. But Dr. Corner advised him to wait until he was at least 40 years old and had earned a reputation by research in some other subject, and also to wait until he could launch his investigations under the impeccable auspices of a major medical school or university.

For ten years, therefore, Dr. Masters built up a solid reputation as a gyne-cologist, publishing 25 contributions on obstetrics and gynecology, including 14 on hormone replacement therapy for post-menopausal women. In 1954, when he was 38 (two years short of the recommended age), he set up a sex research project at the Washington University School of Medicine at St. Louis, Missouri, funded partly by the medical school and partly by a research grant from the U.S. Public Health Service. Ten years later he established his own Reproductive Biology Research Foundation near the medical school campus, financed privately and by various philanthropic foundations.

By 1957 Dr. Masters needed a female assistant. The Washington University Placement Bureau sent him Mrs. Johnson, a married woman with two children but by then separated from her husband. Born in Missouri in 1925, she had originally studied music, later switching to psychology and sociology. According to Dr. Masters she has an incredible facility for personal relationships, an active curiosity, and is prepared to work her head off.

Sexual Histories

In 1954, Dr. Masters had begun his researches by collating the sexual histories of 118 prostitutes whom he had interviewed and who had described, as he put it, "many methods for elevating and controlling sexual tensions and demonstrated innumerable variations in stimulative techniques." In these early researches Dr. Masters laid the foundations of the laboratory methods he was to use in his later observations and recordings: routines were evolved for connecting the various instruments to measure heart rate, brain patterns, muscle tone, temperature, respiration and so on, and for setting up the equipment for filming.

Sex in Four Phases

The panel of subjects for the study of normal sexual responses was chosen from 619 women and 654 men volunteers. After careful screening to weed out exhibitionists, those unable to respond sexually while under observation and those with any history of emotional disturbance, a total of 694 men and women was chosen: 276 of them married couples, plus 106 women and 36 men who were not married when they began the project. The age of the men ranged from 21 to 89; the women from 18 to 78.

The findings of these investigations were collated in *Human Sexual Response,* which became a best seller despite the clinical way in which it was written. Its successor, *Human Sexual Inadequacy,* just as dry in approach, was equally popular. Clearly, Masters and Johnson were answering a generally felt need. What then were their most important findings?

They divided the sexual responses of both men and women into four phases: the excitement phase, most obviously signaled by erection of the penis in men and by moistening of the vagina in women; the plateau phase, which brings other physical changes

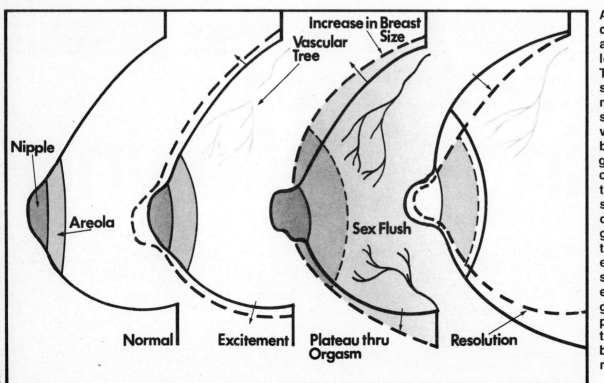

Nipple
Areola
Increase in Breast Size
Vascular Tree
Sex Flush
Normal
Excitement
Plateau thru Orgasm
Resolution

Quartet

A diagram of the breast during sexual arousal and orgasm. At extreme left is the normal breast. The second drawing shows the breast and nipple beginning to swell. Veins called the vascular tree begin to become visibly engorged. The areola, or circle of tissue around the nipple, begins to swell. In the third drawing the breast has grown much larger and the nipple is near full erection. It takes on a sex flush or pink mottling effect. As the breast goes into the resolution phase (extreme right), the nipple and areola begin to recede to normal size.

as sexual excitement increases; the orgasm itself, which releases the muscular tensions and initiates the release of blood from vessels engorged during the preceding cycles, together with the ejaculation of semen in the male orgasm and a series of rhythmic contractions of the vaginal barrel in the female; and the final resolution phase, when the body returns to its normal, unaroused state. In men the resolution phase is accompanied by a refractory period during which they cannot have an erection. But otherwise the four phases are exactly similar in men and women, the same responses occurring in much the same order, regardless of the type of stimulation that evoked them.

These findings are perhaps not startling in themselves, but the research program threw up incidental findings en route which exploded several sexual myths. There is, for example, a widely held belief that penis size is related to sexual performance. Masters and Johnson found that the differences in size are to a very large degree leveled out by erection, a smaller organ increasing in length more impressively than a longer one; in addition, the vagina accommodates the actual penile size, and no more. The combination of these two factors means that the actual size of the penis is usually a minor factor in sexual stimulation of the female partner.

They also disproved Sigmund Freud's theory that there are two kinds of female orgasm, clitoral and vaginal. Their researches showed that there is only one kind of orgasm from a physiological point of view, and that is a sexual orgasm irrespective of how the stimulation has been applied.

The Truth about Sex

The researchers also established that the human female is multi-orgasmic, and able to experience five or six full orgasms within a matter of minutes, which do not differ materially from single orgasms. Masculine endurance rather than feminine responsivity is the limiting factor in a woman's coital responses.

The mutual orgasm as a goal to be striven for is, they say, divisive and distress-producing. If it happens naturally, it is of course a fine thing; but the orgasm is a self-orientated, totally involving experience which reduces the awareness of the partner's response, and there should be no sense of guilt or failure if orgasm does not happen simultaneously. As Mrs. Johnson puts it, "Sex by direction rather than by understanding is not satisfying. It is the give-to-get that makes real response." Over-striving for a mutual orgasm, making mental notes minute by minute to try to keep in step, depersonalizes and dehumanizes the whole experience.

Some of the women became pregnant while taking part in the program. Masters and Johnson were able to observe six of them, supplementing this small sample with 113 volunteers, to compare their responses during pregnancy with their responses at other times. In most respects they were the same; and Masters and Johnson came to the conclusion that for most women there is no reason to refrain from sex during the first three months of pregnancy, or, for the majority of women, during the second three months. For the last three months and the postnatal period the matter of coition should be individualized with the woman's doctor,

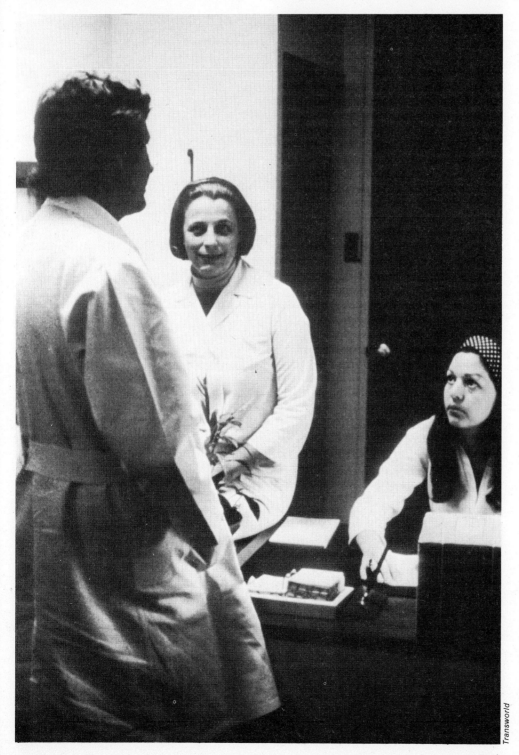

Transworld

Virginia Johnson (center), with colleagues. As Dr. Masters' research associate, she helped him to pioneer research into human sexual response. Their work has allowed the medical profession to help countless men and women to sexual adjustment and happiness.

but in most cases it will be unnecessary to refrain from sex for long periods, such as six weeks before and six weeks after birth.

Female sexual desire, they found, does not normally diminish during pregnancy; or indeed during menstruation or after the menopause. Masters and Johnson brought good news to older people of both sexes: age is not a crucial factor in sexual response; given a good state of health, an interested and interesting partner and continuity of function, there is no reason why sexual activity should not continue with enjoyment into the 60s, 70s and on into the 80s.

The Artificial Vagina

Of vital importance to an extremely distressed minority are their studies on the artificial vagina. There are estimated to be 18,000 women in the United States today born without a vagina, a condition called vaginal agenesis. Surgery can create an artificial vagina, by grafting skin from the thighs or abdomen. In addition Masters and Johnson suggested the use of nonsurgical techniques by the application of a perineal dilator, which by gentle stretching of the small dimple where the vagina should be ultimately creates a vaginal barrel.

During long term follow-ups of detailed physiological and psychological results of the artificial vagina, they found that despite the fact that the artificial vagina is lined with skin, not with a mucous membrane as is a true vagina, over weeks and months the skin lining comes more and more to resemble the lining of a true vagina, and at last even secretes lubricating fluid. In fact, in almost all significant aspects vaginal agenesis patients with artificial vaginas are found to respond to sexual stimulation in precisely the same way as other women; and some conceive and bear children, either by normal means or by Caesarian section.

Abnormal Sex

Masters' and Johnson's work also includes the treatment of sexual inadequacy, or what they call failure of sexual communication, such as impotence, premature ejaculation and female non-orgasm. They report an 80 percent cure rate five years after a two-week treatment at St. Louis. The patients, who have usually been referred to them by their doctor or clergyman, are treated as couples, as Dr. Masters says there is no such thing as a non-traumatized partner in a marriage where there is a complaint

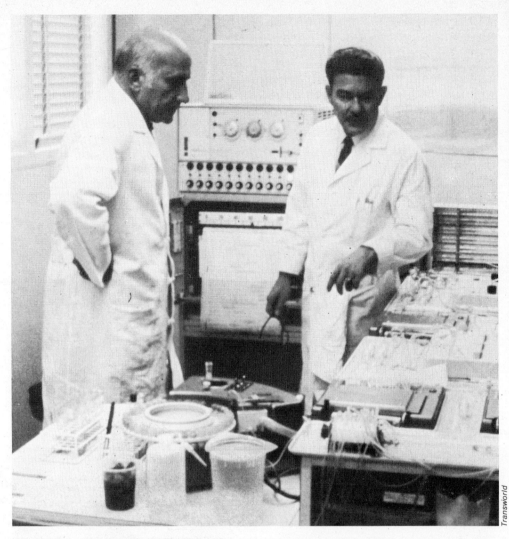

Transworld

Dr. William Masters (left) talks to a colleague. His contribution to the study of human sexuality will be of continuing great value to researchers.

of sexual inadequacy: "The marriage itself is the patient."

Early in the treatment, having spent three days in interviews and physical examination, the couples are required to engage unobserved in what Masters and Johnson call "sensate focus": one at a time, the partners touch each other, avoiding the sexual areas, to discover what pleases the other ("giving to get" again); then they include the sexual areas as well, until coitus follows as a natural development.

Finally they move on to the particular therapy required. In some cases particular positions for coitus will be recommended, or particular techniques, such as the "squeeze technique," applied to the erected penis by the wife to control premature ejaculation. (This problem has been found to be one of the most easily curable conditions: among 186 men treated, only 4 failed to respond during the first two weeks of therapy, and in five years of treatment there was only a single relapse.)

In some cases Masters and Johnson make use of partner surrogates for single or divorced men without a female partner of their own; these are carefully selected volunteers who participate in the physical aspects of the treatment in the same way as a wife would do. Partner surrogates are not, however, provided for women—so far —because Masters and Johnson do not feel that women are psychologically prepared to accept them. Permissiveness has not yet, they think, reached a sufficient depth in female sexuality.

Love-making

Masters and Johnson have also carried out considerable research into homosexuality, focusing particularly on lesbianism. A book on the subject may be expected before this decade is through. When it is published it may well help to reduce as many phobias about "abnormal" sex as their earlier work has done for heterosexuality. At the forefront of their work is the desire to make sex as natural, and enjoyable, a function as eating. "It is," says Mrs. Johnson, "a natural birthright, rather than a thing you use all up, or break, or ruin."